Becc

durin

There was so much more Becca had not told Karen. As much as she was drawn to Barnabas, she was also frightened by her feelings. If she were right, and Barnabas was fond of her, too, what would it mean for the future? Was she prepared to consider staying in Nepal more than one year? Although Barnabas wanted to go to the States to study, he did not want to stay there. She chided herself for jumping ahead of the circumstances. So much remained unspoken between them. The longer she was in Nepal, the more she realized that she had much more to learn about herself, apart from other relationships.

And what about Dan? Was she being fair to him? She was comfortable with Dan and fond of him, but she was neither inspired nor excited by him. Did she need to be challenged in order to love? She struggled with whether she should expect to be provoked by a man or whether she should find her own confrontations within herself. Either choice might mean leaving Dan behind. Was she prepared to do that, after everything she had invested in that relationship?

SUSANNAH HAYDEN is the pen name of a versatile and gifted author of fiction and biography for both adults and children. Susannah makes her home in Colorado Springs with her husband and children.

Books by Susannah Hayden

HEARTSONG PRESENTS
HP14—A Matter of Choice
HP69—Between Love and Loyalty
HP77—The Road Before Me
HP113—Between the Memory and the Moment
HP117—Farther Along the Road
HP134—The Road Home

ROMANCE READER—TWO BOOKS IN ONE
RR9—Summer's Wind Blowing & Spring Waters Rushing

Nepali Noon

Susannah Hayden

Heartsong Presents

A note from the Author:
I love to hear from my readers! You may write to me at the following address:

Susannah Hayden
Author Relations
P.O. Box 719
Uhrichsville, OH 44683

ISBN 1-55748-909-2

NEPALI NOON

Cover illustration by Kay Salem.

PRINTED IN THE U.S.A.

one

"Can you toss me that blue skirt?" Rebecca Masterson held out her hand and waited for her friend, Karen Jacobs, to cast the garment across the bed. As Karen did so, Rebecca's eyes roamed the stacks of clothing cluttering her bed. She would have room for only about half of what she had taken out of the closet.

"I haven't seen you in that skirt in ages," Karen commented. "You always said that it made you look frumpy."

"I know, but. . ." Becca concentrated on folding the skirt and laying it neatly in the large, open suitcase.

"But missionaries are supposed to be frumpy?"

Becca laughed. "No, I wouldn't go so far as to say that. But the literature I got from the mission agency suggested conservative clothing. The women in Nepal still dress in very traditional ways. I've got to keep myself properly covered up."

Karen flopped back on the bed, her hands thrown up over her head. "I still can't believe you're going to a place like Nepal," she said, stretching her legs out to be comfortable.

"Sometimes, neither can I." Becca ran her fingers through her frizzy brown bangs. "If I had known a few weeks ago that I was going to do this, I would never have gotten this silly perm."

"Your hair looks nice. I thought you liked it."

"I do. . .for here. But I don't want to go over there and be some flashy American type. Besides, I'll be gone for a year and this perm will never last that long. Out in the middle of nowhere I won't be able to do anything about it."

"So why are you going? Why the sudden decision to leave the country?"

Becca picked up a beige cardigan and folded it thoughtfully.

"Oh, I don't know exactly." She sat at the foot of the bed and looked across at Karen, her best friend for the last seven years. "Sometimes it doesn't make sense to me at all. I have a good teaching job, a great family. . ."

"You've got a good thing going here," Karen said.

"Well, maybe so. But. . ."

"And Dan."

Becca smiled self-consciously against her will. "Yes, and Dan. But when I read in the church newsletter about the need for a short-term teacher in Nepal, something sprung loose in me. I wanted to go." She stood up and resumed her packing, carefully pushing a pile of skirts to one side of the suitcase. "Actually, I never dreamed I'd be accepted. I've been in shock ever since the phone call came. I have no experience in what they want me to do."

"You're a good teacher."

"Still, they're taking a chance on me. I guess they figure I can't do much damage in just a year."

"Did you ever find out how many children you'll have to teach?"

"Eleven. There are five missionary families at that station. Not all of the children are school age yet, but the eleven who are study together."

"Sounds like an old-fashioned, one-room schoolhouse."

"In a way that's what it is. It'll certainly be a challenge. I'm used to twenty-seven third graders who are all pretty much at the same level. Now my students will range from first grade to seventh."

"I always thought missionaries couldn't get into Nepal."

"Well, they don't write 'missionary' on their visa applications. They are all the types of skilled people the government wants: doctors, engineers, educators."

Karen punched the pillow under her head and was quiet for a moment. "You know, Dan called me as soon as he found out you were going and he wanted me to talk some sense into you."

Becca scrunched up her face. "What?"

Karen nodded and kept talking. "He was really upset at first. I mean, the way he found out, and all."

Becca stiffened. "I didn't mean for him to find out when the pastor announced it to the whole congregation. I tried to tell him for several days. But he was so busy at work. He kept canceling our dates. I wasn't even sure he'd make it to church that morning."

"When he calmed down a bit, I think he realized that," Karen said, more reassuringly. "It's just that. . ."

"I know, Karen, I know."

"I don't know what he thinks is going to happen to you over there, but he didn't want you to go."

"He still doesn't. We spent a lot of time last night, hashing it out."

"Did you come to any agreement?"

"It's my decision. Dan has to understand and respect that."

"But he cares an awful lot about you."

"I know that." Becca looked away from Karen and kept her hands busy.

"Don't you love Dan?"

"Yes, I think I do."

"Everybody thinks you two are going to get married."

Becca shrugged one shoulder. "Yes, I know that, too. And I suppose it's true."

"But you're going to Nepal! What is Dan supposed to think?"

"Whose side are you on, anyway, Karen?" Becca was surprised at the edge she heard in her own voice.

Karen sat up on the bed and faced Becca squarely. "I'm not on anyone's side. It's your life and your choice. It'd be different if you were already married, but you're not."

"Exactly my point."

"But I can understand Dan's feelings, too. He had no way to

see this coming. He's thinking that you're going to get engaged soon. Then suddenly, with two weeks notice, you're leaving for the other side of the world."

"I know, I know," Becca groaned. "Dan is great. And we've talked about marriage lots of times. Eventually we'll get married, I'm sure."

"But. . . ?"

"But I need an adventure first."

"An adventure?" Karen looked sharply at her friend. "You're going to be a missionary because you need an adventure?"

"Doesn't sound too spiritual, I suppose. I didn't mean it quite like that."

"How did you mean it?" Karen gently pressed Becca to be more specific, just as she always had during the years of their friendship.

"Well, I think part of the reason Dan and I haven't gotten married before this is that we're both enjoying our independence. We have our jobs and each other, but we have more latitude than most married people have."

"Marriage is not a prison, you know." Karen threw a stray hand towel at Becca's face.

"I know. You and Phil are deliriously happy, I'm sure," Becca said, theatrically. "You still have that honeymoon glow after a whole year."

"Becca, I don't understand why you're so reluctant to get married. You're going to end up an old maid."

Becca shrugged. "So what if I do?" She grew more thoughtful. "I guess I just want to do something on my own before I settle down and become the wife of a computer whiz who says a lot of things I don't understand because my brain is stalled at the third-grade level."

"Don't you think you're being a little melodramatic?"

"Would you stop with your probing questions?"

"Sorry."

"I've made a decision, and I'm going to stick to it no matter what you and Dan say."

"I guess I'm having as much trouble as Dan is, accepting the fact that you're leaving at six o'clock tomorrow morning."

"Ah, now you're talking sense. I have to be up at four o'clock. So either get busy and help me pack or get out of my way."

Karen swung her legs down over the side of the bed. "I suppose Phil will be wondering where I am."

"And you said marriage is not a prison."

"It's not!" Karen defended herself. "Is it so bad to have somebody care enough about you to wonder where you are and if you are okay?"

"No, of course not."

"I'll worry about you every minute that you're gone."

Becca crossed the room and pulled open a dresser drawer. "Now who's being melodramatic?" She gathered an armful of socks and balanced them until she got back to the bed and could drop them into the suitcase.

"We've been almost inseparable since we met each other seven years ago."

"You managed to separate enough to meet and marry Phil," Becca teased.

"That's not the same. You understand parts of me that he never will."

Becca sat down and looked at her friend. Together, she and Karen had been through the trials of college, multiple nervous first dates, career anxiety. In college they had spent so much time with each other, running around the campus in their jeans and sweat shirts, that some classmates never were quite sure who was who. After graduation they had found jobs in the same city and shared an apartment until Karen married Phil. Even now, they still saw each other at least twice a week.

In the haste of her decision to take the teaching assignment in Nepal and the confusion it caused in her relationship with

Dan, Becca had to admit that she had not thought much about what it would be like to be separated from Karen. A knot formed in her throat.

"Karen, you love Phil and I care deeply for Dan. But you're right, we have something between us that is special. Being apart for a year won't change that." She got up and went to the dresser again, this time collecting hair ties and a sparse supply of jewelry.

"Are you seeing Dan again tonight?" Karen asked.

Becca shook her head. "No, we decided not to. Or rather I did. But I weakened and said he could take me to the airport in the morning."

"Dan? Up at four in the morning?" Karen was incredulous.

Becca nodded. "I know. Hard to believe, huh? But he gave his word he would not oversleep."

❧

The airport was amazingly busy for 5:30 in the morning. Becca had not flown many times in her twenty-five years, so going to the airport was still a curious experience for her. Still half asleep, she watched as people streamed through the wide corridor leading to the gates. Business travelers in suits and carrying attaché cases would stride purposely across the tiled floor, while one young mother struggled alone with a cranky toddler and a heavy bag. At one point Becca got up and tried to help the haggard woman get settled.

The all-night coffee shop brightened up and got ready for the breakfast rush. Middle-aged waitresses with their hair tucked and pinned arrived in pink uniforms that made them look much more foolish than they were. Stray customers straggled in through the restaurant opening and spread out their newspapers in the empty booths, settling in to sip coffee and watch the clock with one eye. As if there were a list of rules posted somewhere, people spaced themselves far enough apart so that no one would bother anyone else.

Becca sat next to Dan in the narrow, black vinyl chair perched on a metal post in the waiting area of Gate 46. On the wall across from them, the minute hand on the clock practically stood still. Becca had been watching the rhythmic jerks of the red second hand marking off their few remaining moments together. Her flight was due to begin boarding any minute now. Becca shuffled her carry-on bag between her ankles for the umpteenth time. Outside, dawn was breaking at last.

Becca would have preferred to have Dan drop her off at the curb with her luggage, but he had insisted on seeing her to the gate and making sure she got on the plane safely. He was strangely protective, as if he had resigned himself to her leaving and was trying to make the most of it, despite his repeated protests of the last two weeks.

As they sat side by side, holding hands awkwardly across the sticky, common armrest, Becca found herself waiting for Dan to again try to persuade her to change her mind. She could hear the lines running through her head. It's not too late. You don't have to get on that plane. The mission can find someone else.

But Dan was silent. Out of the corner of her eye, Becca studied the strained and worried look on his face. His dark hair, cut short for efficiency and to control the unruly wave it acquired when it got long, needed combing. His blue cotton shirt was rumpled with one corner of the collar turned in wrong. Becca smiled at the image. Dan had never been much of a morning person. He had insisted on picking her up at 4:30 in the morning, but he was much too groggy to converse. Instead, he simply sat and held her hand, squeezing it from time to time.

Becca was comfortable just letting him hold her hand if that was what he wanted to do. It had been difficult to say goodbye to her parents in the predawn darkness. The kitchen of the house she had grown up in seemed falsely lit at that hour, as if the whole episode could not be happening in real life. But it was happening. Becca's mind was racing ahead to the long journey she faced: a flight across the U.S. to California, a change of planes for a flight to Bangkok with a stopover in Tokyo, and on to Katmandu. New people, new places, new languages—everything would be fresh and invigorating. Her travelers' guide on Nepal and an emergency vocabulary list stuck out the pocket of her carry-on bag. *Namaste*, she said in her mind, and tried to visualize herself putting her palms together and bowing to someone she might meet in Nepal.

Finally, her flight was called. Suddenly nervous, she got up to join the boarding line. Still holding her hand, Dan stayed with her until she handed her ticket to the flight attendant. As she hoisted her carry-on bag to her shoulder, he abruptly pulled her close and kissed her longingly—and with enough tenderness to make Becca have fleeting second thoughts about her decision.

When they parted, he said hoarsely, "Goodbye, Becca."

"I'll see you in a year," Becca said, suddenly wanting to lighten the mood between them. She intertwined her fingers with his in a conciliatory gesture.

Dan simply nodded. "In a year." With one last stroke of her arm, he turned and walked away, leaving her to walk the gangway to the plane and find her seat.

two

Becca lost count of the hours that had passed since she last slept. On the flight from Los Angeles to Bangkok, she wedged into the middle seat of her row, with the knees of a very tall, very intimidating man pushed up into her back. Reclining was impossible. Her pillow would not stay behind her neck. The woman next to her insisted on keeping her light on. By the time the flight landed in Tokyo for a one-hour layover, Becca wished she had splurged on a first class ticket where there might have been at least a remote chance of dozing off occasionally.

As it was, she shuffled through the plane change in Bangkok with an enormous headache. The din and echoing chaos of the great hall where all passengers had to check in and go through customs were overwhelming. As tired as she was, Becca could barely sift through the sounds and signs to decide which instructions applied to her. Once, in line for the X-ray machine, she tried to sit on her suitcase for a few moments. But she soon felt as if she might be smothered in the crowd if she did not stand up and stake out her territory. She heard countless languages around her in the international terminal. Every now and then she heard snatches of English and found herself craning her neck toward a passing conversation.

In the smaller airport in Katmandu, she stood in yet another line, her passport and immigration card in hand. The line hardly seemed to move, but at least it was not as crowded as Bangkok had been.

Looking around her, she saw a mixture of travelers: Nepalis with the self-confidence of being in their own country, Indian women with their colorful saris, even a group of about twenty

Tibetan monks with their shaved heads and orange robes. In such a setting it was easy to spot the Americans and Europeans, outfitted with hiking boots and backpacks. Obviously they were there to enjoy trekking in the picturesque Himalayas. Within a few weeks, they would be back in their own countries, in their own homes, regaling their friends with stories and photographs of their adventures.

Becca shoved her bag forward with her foot and moved up a few steps. *And what about my adventure?* she wondered. Her shoulders sagged under the weight of her carry-on bag and the realization that she had left her comfortable home and friends for something completely unknown. She was not as adventurous as she had led Karen to believe two days ago. And she would not be home in just a few weeks. Instead, she would be finishing up a crash course introducing her to the Nepali language and culture. From there, she would go to the remote mountain village where she would spend the next eleven months living and working. *What have I done?* she asked herself with irrational fright. *I don't even like to go camping for the weekend.*

At the moment, none of it sounded very glamorous or adventurous. What she wanted most was to soak for at least an hour in a tub of hot water and sink into a bed made up with crisp, clean sheets. She had no doubt that she could sleep for at least twelve hours if she could just lie down anywhere, it did not matter where at this point. The airport floor was beginning to look appealing. Her head throbbed incessantly. She had some painkillers in her bag, but no water. She knew enough not to drink tap water in a foreign country but she had not stopped to buy any bottled water along the way. If she could just get through the visa line, maybe the main area of the airport would offer a restaurant or small shop where someone would speak English, she hoped.

She leaned out to one side to see if she could catch a glimpse of what was on the other side of the immigration booths. All she saw was a dimly lit concrete stairwell.

Vainly, Becca rubbed her temples with her fingertips. She was not unfamiliar with headaches, but this was different. Nothing in the book about jetlag had prepared her for how she felt right now. She had looked at her reflection in the restroom at the Bangkok airport and hardly recognized herself. Despite her best efforts, her permed hair had a mind of its own, and the clothes that she had been wearing continuously for the last two days were stuck to her skin in places. But she was beyond caring about any of that. If someone had picked her up and thrown her against a brick wall, she doubted that she would feel any worse.

Finally her turn came. She pushed her passport across the counter and wearily looked the immigration officer in the eyes. He glanced at her photograph disinterestedly, then at her face, then back to the photograph. With an official gesture, he stamped the document that would admit her to this strange country and waved her through.

Becca entered the concrete stairwell and followed the flow of traffic. Upstairs she encountered more lines and hundreds of people. Hopefully one of the lines would lead to her large suitcase. She had lost track of the Americans she had seen downstairs and was swallowed up in a sea of Asians: Indians, Chinese, Nepalis. As she watched them chatter and gesture, she felt conspicuous in her American clothing, disheveled though it was. And she despaired of learning to communicate. Her total exposure to foreign language had been two years of high school Spanish and she had not taken those courses too seriously. How was she going to learn a language like Nepali in only a few weeks?

The mission agency had assured her that Nepali was not a difficult language to learn, once she got used to the script writing rather than the Phoenecian alphabet. They also reminded her that she would be living in a nearby community with five missionary families who were fluent in the language. No one expected her to master Nepali in one month of language school. Still, she felt overwhelmed.

At last she found her large gray bag and heaved it off the carousel. It had definitely taken a beating during its global journey, but she was glad to see it had arrived intact. She heaved it off the revolving strip and plopped it onto the steady floor.

Becca was not sure what to do next. The mission had promised that someone would meet her at the airport, but so far she had not noticed anyone who seemed to be looking for her. Lugging her suitcase behind her, she once again followed the drift of the crowd and moved away from the luggage area. As she turned toward the door leading out of the building, she searched frantically for signs that someone was meeting her. Bravely, she started walking toward the door.

"Rebecca Masterson? Is that you?" A British, female voice somehow broke through the confusion and reached Becca's ears.

Becca turned to see a fiftyish, gray-haired woman looking at her expectantly. "Yes, that's me. I'm Becca." Immediately she realized how distraught she sounded. "I'm sorry if I sound anxious. I'm just so tired."

"Jetlag," the woman said with a note of experience. "Turns you inside out every time." She put out her hand. "I'm Harriett Metcalf. We're awfully glad you made it in today."

"So am I."

Harriett took the large bag from Becca and motioned toward the door. "I've got a taxi waiting," she said, "but we must hurry."

Becca followed Harriett's pear-shaped form covered in a flower-print dress. Harriett wore sturdy, flat sandals and moved with the self-confidence of an experienced career missionary who had long ago become accustomed to this place. Becca's eyes focused on the taxi waiting for them—an old, rusted, compact car that would probably not be allowed on the streets in the U.S. It was so dirty she was not even sure what the color was supposed to be. Beige? White? Gray? As the driver respectfully nodded at her and took her bags, she inspected the back seat through the window. She could feel her allergies kicking in just looking at the dust inside the car, with its cracked vinyl seats and worn carpet. Every car at the airport looked like a variation of this same model. *My father would have a fit if he saw me getting into a rattletrap like this*, she thought with a wave of homesickness.

The driver opened the door and gestured that she should get in. Harriett nudged her from behind. "Come on, he needs to move the car."

Inside, Becca gripped the seat as the driver jerked his way into the flow of traffic. All around them drivers blared their horns and resisted slowing down for any reason at all. Becca could not see the speedometer, but common sense told her that the taxi was moving too fast for the congested traffic. As they approached a major intersection, Becca scanned the area for a traffic light, but there was none. She gripped the seat more tightly.

"We'll be at the mission house in only a few minutes," Harriett was saying. Becca suddenly realized she had not been paying attention to Harriett at all. "Dinner is at half past five. That'll give you a chance to meet the others who are in town for language school."

Becca wearily nodded acknowledgment.

"Don't worry, Rebecca," Harriett said, patting Becca's hand. "You will get to sleep, I promise you."

"I'm dying for a bath," Becca admitted to her new friend. "I could soak for hours."

Harriett chuckled. "I'm afraid you'll have to wait a bit on that. We have showers only at the mission's guest house, and even they are not what you are used to."

Becca's disappointment was obvious. "Well, the main thing is to get cleaned up, I guess."

❧

Becca stared at the mounted water heater in the cement-walled bathroom she shared with a Finnish family of five. *Shouldn't there be a red light or something?* she wondered. *How do I know it's working?* Harriett had warned her that it would take thirty minutes to heat up enough water to take a shower.

Harriett had fixed Becca a cup of tea as soon as they reached the mission's guest house. The hot drink had helped a little with her headache, making her realize how hungry she was. Her last meal on the plane was a dim memory. Despite her appetite, she was almost too tired to move. Her arms felt like dead weights strapped to her torso, and she was afraid she would fall over unconscious at the dinner table.

Somehow, Becca had made it through the evening meal, where fifteen other missionaries and children gathered to recap their day and find out about the newest house member. Some had been in the country for years and were passing through the guest house on their way out for a furlough. Others had been there only a few weeks, studying the language as Becca soon would. One couple, who worked in a remote mountain village, was there to await the birth of their third child.

Becca was the only American. The others were a mixture of Europeans, which surprised Becca. She chided herself for her narrow-minded thinking that all missionaries were Americans.

Only Harriett and her husband lived at the guest house all year round. The others were as transitory as Becca. Yet they had formed their own community within the walls of the mission compound. Becca looked on, as if she were peering through the glass of a candy counter, yearning for sweet treasures. Would she come to feel a part of this group? Would she come to believe she could do something valuable in Nepal, something that justified her presence? She answered the questions asked of her, but for the most part she was too sleepy to engage in conversation. As soon as she could politely do so, she excused herself and went upstairs to clean up.

Now, standing in the bathroom, at last she was only minutes away from being able to sink into a bed. It was barely seven o'clock in the evening, but having lost an entire night's sleep and traveled halfway around the world, Becca was oblivious to time. She simply wanted to sleep.

She peeled off her clothes in layers and let them fall to a heap on the bathroom floor. For the first time she wondered about laundry facilities. When would she be able to wash her traveling clothes? Tentatively she turned on the water and made sure the tall waste basket was nearby. Harriett had suggested that she save her shower water as much as possible; she would need it for flushing the toilet. Becca had been reluctant to admit she did not know how to use shower water to flush the toilet. She would have to figure that out later.

The water was cold. Sticky from the warm day, Becca waved her hands in the water and waited for it to warm up. She adjusted the knobs and waited some more. Nothing seemed to help. Cold water trickled out, battling vainly for sufficient pressure to work up a spray. Despite her dutiful, thirty-minute wait, Becca saw no sign she was going to be rewarded with hot water.

Nearly in tears, she considered her alternatives. She could just go to bed and try again in the morning, but that did not seem too appealing for she really wanted to wash away the toil of her journey. Besides, she had already invested a precious half-hour waiting for the water and anticipating the sensation of being clean once again. Taking a deep breath, she stepped into the cold stream. Gasping, she rapidly washed and rinsed and turned off the water as soon as possible.

She reached for her pajamas and robe and dressed herself, letting her sopping hair hang loose. Gingerly she gathered up her clothing from the floor, picked up her cosmetic bag, and opened the bathroom door. After peering out to make sure no one was in the hall, she took quick steps to her own room and dropped onto the bed.

The room was small, with a bare linoleum floor, one bed, a desk with several gouges, and a standing wardrobe cabinet. With her suitcase in one corner of the floor, Becca barely had space to turn around. This was home for the next six weeks. She took off her robe and made a feeble attempt to comb through her hair before giving in to her exhaustion.

As she lay on the bed, Becca had the fleeting feeling that this was all a dream. She would waken in the morning and discover herself home in her own apartment in Porter. The phone would ring and Dan would ask if she wanted to go out for breakfast.

Becca pulled a light blanket up around her neck and sank into oblivion.

three

To Becca's dismay, she did not sleep for twelve hours. Barely five hours passed before she was wide awake. A look at her glowing wristwatch told her that back home in Porter it was late morning, usually her most alert time of day. Defying the logic of her exhausting journey, her mind was wakeful and restless for stimulation. Becca reached for the lamp switch and sighed in gratitude when it responded. The small bulb gave a yellowish cast to the area around the head of the bed, a strange circle of security in her midnight isolation.

Sleeping problems were new to Becca and she was not sure what she was supposed to do. Get up and exercise to wear herself out? Find something boring to read until drowsiness returned? Turn off the light and force herself to go back to sleep? Despite the state of her mind, her body was too tired for exercise. But she was too awake to think that simply turning off the light would allow her to go back to sleep. Reading seemed the best alternative, but Becca had not allocated any precious luggage space to leisure reading. All of the literature she had brought pertained to her new teaching job.

Becca remembered seeing a bookcase stuffed with paperbacks down in the dining room. She would have to leave the refuge of her room and find her way downstairs in the dark, so she almost opted to just turn off the light and lie quietly in bed. But she told herself she was being silly and swung her legs over the side of the bed and put on her bathrobe.

The stairwell was shadowy, though not completely dark. Outside the door of the Finnish family's room, she thought she heard a baby stir from within and she made an effort to be extra quiet as she continued her nocturnal exploration. Becca saw no sign that anyone else was awake. In the dining room, she groped along the wall until she encountered a light switch. The room filled with light, alarming Becca. She did not want to discard the reality of night so brazenly. Quickly she located a table lamp, then turned off the overhead lights.

Being up in the middle of the night, creeping around unfamiliar surrounds, was unsettling. If she occasionally prowled around her own apartment at night, or even her parents' living room, she was in her own territory, free to do as she wished with the items she encountered. But here, she was oddly afraid to touch anything.

Next to the couch was a stack of American and European magazines: *Better Homes and Gardens*, *Ladies' Home Journal*, *Newsweek*, and an assortment of others. Becca stepped over and quietly flipped through them. Some were nearly five years old but it was clear from their condition that they were well-used, regardless of their age. Becca pondered their significance, the connection to the cultures from which missionaries came. Some missionaries lived their whole adult lives outside of their own cultures, Becca knew. Even in the context of such a commitment, occasionally they wanted news of their home countries, something to read from their original cultures. Even an old magazine would do.

Becca knew very little about Nepal. It was a small, faraway country that had no relevance to her daily existence. Three weeks earlier, she would have been hard pressed to find it on a map. She could not conceive of coming to such a place intending to spend a lifetime, even with the benefit of years of preparation instead of the quick introductory course she would undergo.

Becca put the magazines down and turned to the bookcase, the reason she had come downstairs in the first place. She quickly saw she had her choice between serious classic novels, recent U.S. bestsellers, and light romance. Most of the bestsellers she had already read, so she took a thick, John Steinbeck novel and a thin romance. Surely one or the other would help her pass the time.

Upstairs again, two more hours passed before the fatigue of her body caught up with her brain and Becca slept again.

When she awoke six hours later, it was Saturday morning. At breakfast, the dining room was once again a jumbled cultural exchange. The German couple was at the maternity hospital; the wife had gone into labor early in the morning.

"Good morning, Becca," Harriett Metcalf greeted her enthusiastically and gestured to an empty chair. "Did you sleep well?"

"While I slept, I slept well. But I was awake for several hours during the night."

Harriett nodded knowingly. "That may go on for several days, even a week. But you'll get turned around eventually. Juice?"

Becca nodded and Harriett filled her glass. She saw toast and jam, cereal, and raisins on the table before her, and suddenly Becca was ravenously hungry.

"We were just discussing church," Harriett said. "Charlie and I usually go to an English service, but some of the others are going to a Nepali church. You're welcome to go along."

"Today?" Becca asked, confused because it was Saturday.

"Sunday is a work day here," someone explained, "so most of the Christians worship on Saturday."

Becca nodded, understanding. "Is it far?"

"We can walk, but we'll have to leave in about ten minutes."

Becca bit into a piece of toast. "I'll be ready."

On the ride from the airport the day before, Becca had experienced the traffic of Katmandu from inside the relative safety of the taxi. The pedestrian viewpoint was entirely different. The group of six set out as a block, but soon they had to walk single file along the narrow road. The road to the church curved up a gradual hill. It was unpaved and dust swirled up with every step they took. This particular stretch of road was too narrow for the city buses to pass, hemmed in by the brick walls surrounding small houses. But taxis and personal vehicles swarmed while bicyclists cut in and out of traffic in a seemingly careless, random way. Becca was on edge with every step. Horns and bells beeped in short patterns that apparently were meaningful to everyone except Becca.

They entered a more open area of shops and racks of wares displayed on the sidewalk. A narrow strip of cement provided a measure of security for pedestrians, and Becca was able to look at something other than where she would put her foot down next.

Becca was quite taken with the colorful bolts of fabrics and intricately woven rugs and had begun to find the walk delightful. She began formulating ideas for gifts she would purchase later to take home to family and friends. However, when she saw the goat's head protruding from the end of a stick, she nearly stopped breathing. Actually there were three heads—six eyes staring blankly out of heads that were complete except for having been separated from their bodies. She looked away, shuddering to think what might be inside that shop.

Turning a corner, they walked past a row of small houses and came to the church, a longish, orange brick building with a door on one side at the back. In the safekeeping of her group, Becca approached the door and then saw the pile of shoes outside it. With the deftness that comes from habit, everyone entering the church slipped off their shoes and set them on the wooden racks. When the racks were full, they piled shoes, unconcerned, on the ground and proceeded in for worship.

Inside, the single large room was nearly full. Women and children sat on one side, men on the other. A few older people and a pregnant missionary sat on wooden chairs against the back wall. The rest of the 300 worshippers sat on rugs and pieces of carpet spread out on the cement floor. Becca and her companions found places near the back. They were soon penned in on all sides as the stream of worshipers continued. A mother and three children pressed into a small empty space next to Becca, separating her from the others in her group. Becca pulled her knees up to her chest to make more room.

Although Becca could not understand any of the words around her, she quickly caught the spirit of the service. They stood for a long time, singing and clapping, and again later to pray. Everyone prayed aloud at once, raising their hands, their voices swelling and fading and swelling again with words of gratitude and praise. Becca watched in awe. She had gone to church all her life, but she had never seen a group of Christians so unabashed and free in their worship, and this in a country that until very recently was hostile to Christianity and in which it was still technically illegal to encourage anyone to change religions.

Becca was fascinated with one young man who helped to lead the singing. From the back of the room, she could not see his features clearly but every time he leaned in toward the microphone to start off a new song, she craned her neck for a better look. He was slight of build, like many of the Nepali men she had seen so far, with longish black hair and a full beard. When he sang, he closed he eyes reverently and pleasurably, giving himself over completely to his worship. Smooth and mellow, his voice poured through the sound system and settled sweetly on Becca's ears. She did not know what he was singing; she did not need to know. His voice and demeanor, even in front of a crowd, were so transparent that even without words Becca saw the purity of his devotion.

Suddenly she was conscious of being a spectator when she ought to have been a worshiper. She opened up her English Bible and began to read some psalms.

The pastor stood to read from the Bible and the room became quiet. Except for the youngest of children, the congregation listened raptly as the Word of God was read. Then the sermon began. Becca did not known know the topic of the sermon, but she tried to listen dutifully and devoutly.

Despite her best intentions, her attention wandered. In her peripheral vision she was aware of a repeated motion outside the door and she turned her head toward it. A woman, wrinkled and brown and ancient looking, was reorganizing the shoes. At her direction, two teen-age boys carried in an empty rack and resituated the existing ones. The woman found small openings for children's thongs, shifted tennis shoes and sandals around, and hammered away at her project. She would make a few adjustments, pick up a pair of shoes from the pile, and make more adjustments. To Becca it seemed like a pointless task. She was convinced the old woman would never find enough empty places for all the shoes and, when the service was over and everyone came out, no one would know where their shoes were. Becca made sure she kept track of where her own shoes were put. Obviously the church needed more shoe racks to accommodate its growth; what the woman was doing would have little impact for the long term.

Still, Becca was impressed that she was doing something. She worked steadily and authoritatively, undaunted by the seeming impossibility of the task.

The sermon lasted a long time. The pastor preached with energy and purpose; that much Becca could tell, despite the language barrier. She tried to make some sense of what he said, at least to listen for patterns in his language and identify words or phrases that he repeated. But she made little progress. She only hoped that in six weeks, when she was due to leave Katmandu, Nepali would not seem like such a chaotic tangle of sounds.

Her eyes went almost cyclically from the preacher, to the open Bible in her lap, to the woman working steadily outside the door. To Becca's amazement, the woman made great progress. By the time the sermon finished, every pair of shoes had its place and they fit perfectly together.

As the pastor finished praying, he formed a set of sounds Becca recognized. "Barnabas." The young man who had led the singing early in the service stepped forward. *Ah*, Becca thought. *His name is Barnabas*. She watched as he confidently moved to the microphone to begin the song that would end the service. His eyes remained open this time and surveyed the people of the congregation as they sang. Then they settled on Becca. She told herself that it was impossible that he was really looking at her. She was one person among hundreds, standing in the back of the long room. Her stomach flipped in an odd way.

four

Two days later, Becca pulled open the tall, wooden door and entered her language classroom for the first time. It did not look much like a classroom, at least not to someone whose profession was teaching. The room was long and narrow, and the ceiling was high and dark. Wooden beams crisscrossed an intricate green and gold painted design. Electric light bulbs dangled from thin wires, but they did little to brighten the place. Heavy draperies covered the windows, making it difficult even for daylight to penetrate the room.

Becca knew that the large, three-storied building, built around a central courtyard, had originally been the palace of a well-known Nepali prince of 200 years ago. The decorating scheme of that era remained, although decades ago the government converted the building into an academic facility. Twelve student chairs, placed in three neat rows, were the only evidence that the room functioned as a center of learning, Becca was used to her classroom with bulletin boards and chalkboards and fluorescent lights. She was dubious about actually learning anything in a setting such as this one. Yet the school had an excellent reputation for teaching the basics of the Nepali language and culture in a compressed period of time. For now, she would give her instructor the benefit of the doubt.

The old wooden door creaked open and a woman in a wraparound denim skirt and plain white blouse entered. She carried a boxful of books. "Good morning," she said, setting her books on a table in the back of the room. "You must be Rebecca Masterson." She spoke with a distinctly Midwestern accent, which Becca was glad to hear.

"Yes, that's right. And you're Patricia Timbers?"

"Correct. Your teacher for the next six weeks." Patricia began distributing books to half a dozen desks. "I hope you're prepared to work hard. This is not a course for quitters."

Becca was taken a bit off guard by this direct approach. Rapidly she recovered her senses. "Of course. I'll work as hard as I can. How did you know who I was?"

"You're the only woman signed up for the course this time."

"Really? Who are the others?"

"Mostly Europeans coming to work on government contracts. There's one other American. He's a doctor who's going work in a government village health project." Patricia stopped to look Rebecca over. "I understand you're a missionary."

"Well, I'm a teacher," Becca said, hesitant to consider herself a missionary. "I'm here to teach some missionary children for a year."

"They told me you were going out to one of the villages."

"Yes, that's right, in western Nepal."

"It's pretty rough out there. I hope you're prepared."

Once again, Becca did not know what to say. She was spared this time by the entrance of two European men, some of her fellow students. Within a few minutes, the group had assembled. There were six students all together: three German engineers, one English agriculturalist, the American doctor, and Rebecca. After brief introductions, Patricia began in a forthright way to explain what their life would be like for the next four weeks. In the morning and early afternoon, they would study language. In the later part of the day, they would have lectures in Nepali history or cultural field trips. This would include some outings where they would have to maneuver around Katmandu by their own wits. They should expect at least three hours of homework every evening. As Patricia rattled off the things they would be working on, Becca tried to take notes, but she could not keep up. Even after three days, she still felt turned inside out by jetlag much of the time. It was difficult to concentrate. But she would have to concentrate to keep up with Patricia Timbers.

"You'll each have a language tutor," Patricia was saying. "You'll spend part of every day with your tutor working on tonal pronunciation and basic vocabulary. This will give you a chance to practice some of the phrases you will need to get around the city."

As if on cue, the door opened and a line of six Nepali people filed into the room and took seats against a side wall. These were the tutors. A young woman dressed in a beautiful green silk sari led the line. Her eyes met Becca's, and the woman smiled slightly, putting Becca at ease. As she looked from one tutor to the next, Becca caught her breath. The last tutor was the young man from church the other day. At least she thought it was him; she had not seem him this close up.

"Becca, you'll work with Barnabas," Patricia said, nodding toward the young man. "He's interested in going to America one day. I'm sure you'll get along quite well."

As Patricia continued making tutor assignments, Becca, trying not to appear too curious, eyed Barnabas. He was the only one without a Nepali name. His face was covered by a dark, full beard, and his dark eyes sparkled mysteriously from deep in their sockets.

"Let's take a break for lunch now," Patricia said. "They are expecting us in the dining room downstairs. I would suggest that you each eat with your tutor and take advantage of this chance to get to know each other."

The students paired off with their tutors, descended the stairs, and crossed the courtyard to the dining room. Becca smiled awkwardly at Barnabas, not sure how to begin a conversation with him or whether Nepali customs allowed a woman to shake hands with a man. They went through the line together and picked up their tin plates heaped with a rice and curry dish garnished with a few over-cooked vegetables. Up until now, Becca had taken all of her meals at the mission guest house and had not encountered typical Nepali food. The plate held much more than she thought she could eat. The aroma told her that it would be spicy, so she reached for a tin water cup. Taped to an urn was the comforting sign: BOILED WATER. She filled her cup and followed Barnabas to a table.

Before he began to eat, Barnabas bowed his head for a brief moment.

Self-consciously she picked up a fork and took a timid bite of rice.

"Do you like our food?" Barnabas asked, smiling slightly.

Becca blushed. "Actually this is the first time I have had it. I like curry, though. And I like rice. So I suppose I'll like them mixed together."

"To enjoy our food, you must like a great deal of curry and rice," he joked, as he filled his own mouth.

Involuntarily, Becca reached for her water. The spices were strong. She swallowed the water gratefully, both because it put out the fire in her mouth and because Barnabas was pretending not to notice her problem as he added red hot sauce to his own plate. Would she ever get used to this? she wondered. Did the missionaries in her village eat traditional Nepali food? She decided to change the subject.

"How long have you been involved with the language school?" she asked.

"About two years."

"How did you get started?" She inspected her rice for some with less curry.

"I studied English in school. I wanted to improve my English, so I applied to be a tutor. They are very gracious to always match me up with an American student."

"Your English is very good," Becca commented sincerely. Obviously Barnabas was an intelligent and hard-working young man.

"Thank you. Perhaps after one month I will tell you that your

Nepali is also very good."

Becca laughed. "I would be very surprised. I've never had to learn another language before. I'm not sure how well I will do."

"It is my job to see that you do very well. And I am very good at my job."

Becca smiled at his confidence. She knew that tutoring was only part-time work. Surely Barnabas was involved in other work as well. "I'm afraid I might keep you quite occupied," she said. "But I would not want to keep you from other things."

"My job is very flexible."

So he did have a job. "What kind of work do you do?"

"I help to prepare radio programs and cassette tapes."

"Oh? What kind of programs?"

"Religious information."

Becca perked up. "Oh, really?" Then she let her guard down. "I have to confess that I have seen you before. I was at your church on Saturday. You have a beautiful voice."

"I saw you, too," Barnabas said, dropping his eyes.

So Becca had not been subject to an overly active imagination. "The church was very full," she said. "I was not expecting so many Christians in one place."

"We are growing more every day, although in the villages it is much harder to spread the Good News. We are grateful for missionaries like you who come to help us."

Becca decided she was going to have to get used to being considered a missionary, though she still thought of herself simply as a teacher.

"You will like the village where you are going," Barnabas said. "I know the place. The air is much cleaner than Katmandu."

Obviously Barnabas had been given thorough background information on Becca. She wondered what else he already knew about her.

"Have you been to that village?" she asked.

"Several times. I take cassette tapes to the villages so that the people can learn about Jesus."

Becca thought about the lack of electricity she had been told to expect. "Do they have the equipment to play tapes?"

"We take a tape recorder and batteries with us. If there is a Christian in the village, we may leave the equipment there. Then the people come to listen to the tapes whenever they want. Many people in the villages never learn to read, so tapes are more practical than literature."

"I have not seen the villages yet, but I understand they are difficult to travel to. Do you walk everywhere you go?"

"For now we have to walk up the mountains," Barnabas said. "But I have a dream that someday we will be able to travel much more quickly."

"A truck?" Becca guessed.

"No. There are no roads. I want to fly an airplane. Then we can go straight to the top of the mountain if we need to."

"Is there a flight school here? In Katmandu?"

Barnabas shook his head. "I will go the U.S. to learn to fly. I want to be an excellent pilot and learn mechanics, also. This will take several years. But in the mountains, a pilot is useless if he cannot also keep the plane running."

"I never thought of it that way. When are you going to the U.S.?"

"God has not told me yet. There are certain obstacles."

"Obstacles?" Becca hoped she was not being too forward in pressing him, but she was curious.

"My family wants me to be a pilot, and my father is able to pay for the training. But there is something they want me to do first, and I cannot do it."

Becca suppressed the urge to question further but hoped he would keep talking.

"Before I can go to the United States, I must get married. My parents are Hindus and they insist that I take a Hindu wife. But I am a Christian."

"Oh." The complexity of the problem sank in quickly. "Your father wants you to be a pilot, but not so you can fly to the mountaintops."

"He thinks I will make a good income flying for the national airline or for government officials."

"I see." Becca did not know what else to say.

Barnabas smiled. "Do not be concerned. God wants me to be a pilot and He will make the way smooth, just as He has for you. Tell me how you came to know you should come to Nepal."

"It all happened very quickly," Becca said. "I first heard about the position a few weeks ago. Something inside me pushed me to apply. I didn't really think I would be accepted. But I was, and here I am."

"An obedient servant," Barnabas commented.

Becca avoided meeting his eyes. Already she knew how deeply he was convinced that he should spend his life serving God. What would he think if he knew she had started out looking for adventure? Obedience had little to do with her decision to come to Nepal.

"Shall I get you some tea?" Barnabas asked.

Loaded with milk and sugar, tea in Nepal was very different than what Becca preferred, but she did not want to be impolite. She accepted the tea, and they talked about the sites in Katmandu. Becca accepted an invitation to visit a church again with Barnabas on Saturday.

Becca glanced at her watch as she drained her teacup. "We have a few minutes before class starts again. I think I'll take a quick walk."

"You won't find any fresh air in Katmandu," Barnabas warned.

Becca smiled. "I'll stay on the grounds, I promise."

She left him and headed out to the perimeter of the old palace wall. She was not anxious to be walking the streets of Katmandu alone, but she felt she needed a few moments to herself before beginning what promised to be an intense afternoon. Staying inside its confines, she followed the wall around in a clockwise direction.

The garden behind the building sloped gently upward, beckoning toward the foothills of the Himalayas. Before leaving home, Becca had purchased a colorful book of photographs taken in Nepal. The Himalayas appeared on many of its pages: brilliant, snowcapped, enormous. As she lifted her eyes to the hills, Becca now wondered if the Himalayas were really there. The unregulated pollution of Katmandu Valley left a thick, gray blanket in the air, trapped by the height of the surrounding foothills. It was difficult to see to the end of the street, much less into the mountains.

Nevertheless, Becca peered toward the west. Somewhere out there, she was not sure where, was her village and the eleven children who had provided the excuse for her adventure. As strange as Katmandu seemed now, she knew it would seem like a modern metropolis compared to the mountain village for which she was headed.

She did not have to stay. She could repay the mission for her airfare and go home tomorrow. Then she would not have to face the real missionaries with her less-than-sincere motives for coming. She would not have to face Barnabas and squirm under his convictions of God's leading.

"Lord," she murmured, "I can't see the hills, but they are out there, and they are Your hills. I will lift up my eyes to the hills and You will give me strength."

No, she would not leave. She would go back to the classroom and pay close attention to everything that Patricia Timbers said and seek as much help as she could from Barnabas.

five

Becca pushed through the screen door and let her books fall onto the nearest table in the guest house dining room. She was exhausted. After two weeks of language school, she was over her jetlag and used to her daily routine. But she had not been sleeping soundly. At night her mind buzzed with Nepali vocabulary and grammar. She was making good progress; both Patricia and Barnabas thought so. But studying consumed all her energy and time. She was not accustomed to coping with insomnia.

With her arms lightened, she fell into the old, soft sofa against the wall under the window and leaned her head back. She had thirty minutes before Barnabas would come for her and take her on her first Katmandu bus ride. Her intention was to change clothes and freshen up, but she seriously considered just sitting on the couch with her eyes closed. It would be so easy to just fade away for a few minutes. She felt her breathing slow down.

"I see we're a bit tired today."

Becca jumped at the sound of Harriett Metcalf's voice. Involuntarily she blinked and rubbed her eyes. "I guess I should never have sat down," Becca said. "Now I'm not so sure I can get up again."

"Maybe these will perk you up," Harriett said, handing her two white envelopes.

"Mail? I got mail?"

"Looks that way. Enjoy." Harriett turned back to her office work.

Becca held one envelope in each hand: one from her friend, Karen, one from her boyfriend, Dan. She had been in Nepal only two and a half weeks and was not expecting any mail to reach her at the guest house. They must have written as soon as she left. She looked from one to the other, not sure whose letter to open first. Finally, she set Dan's in her lap and tore open Karen's.

Dear Wandering Rebecca,

You've been gone only one day and I miss you already! I keep wanting to pick up the phone to tell you something. Then I remember you are halfway around the world.

I still can't believe you've done this! When we last talked, I probably sounded unconvinced about your adventure theory. But I hope you find adventure this year—and much more. Whatever it takes for you to be happy, that's what I want for you. I'll be waiting to hear the details as only you can tell them.

Phil and I had lunch with Dan today. He looked like a little lost puppy. Phil says it was because he had been up since four in the morning, but I don't think so. He's used to having you around, just like I am. We sat around imagining what Katmandu is like. Write soon! And send pictures so we can visualize where you are.

Love you lots,

Karen

Becca smiled and sighed. She had missed Karen terribly. If they were together, Karen would know everything that had happened in the last two weeks, every feeling, every thought. How different things were now. For the next twelve months, she would have no Karen and no Dan in whom to confide. She was on her own to cope with all the adjustments that lay ahead of her. Most of her adventure was yet to come. Life in the village would be much more rugged than Katmandu. She had very little information about the students she would be teaching or what books or worksheets would be available. Probably there would be no blackboard and she would be holding classes on someone's back porch. Her traditional classroom approaches might not even be suited to children growing up in a foreign country. She had carried in her luggage a selection of teacher guides that she hoped would meet her needs.

Becca picked up Dan's letter, taking comfort in the familiar handwriting that always looked slightly stilted. She thought he tried too hard to make his writing perfect—but that was consistent with his personality. Dan tried to make everything perfect, whether it could be or not. That included their relationship. He had a plan, an agenda, for everything they did. Becca countered by being spontaneous and, according to Dan, sometimes flighty. No doubt he saw her departure for Nepal as one of her flighty decisions.

Dan must have written the same day as Karen. What could he have to say that he had been unable to say at the airport on the morning of her departure? She knew Dan well enough not to expect an emotional goodbye scene. That was not his style. In fact, Becca was surprised he had written at all. She opened the envelope.

Dear Becca,

I can't remember the last time I was up at four in the morning, and I certainly don't look forward to doing it again any time in the near future! But I was glad to be with you and see that you got on the plane all right. I'm assuming no news is good news and that you arrived safely in Katmandu. Jetlag must have you feeling much worse than I do, so I'll complain no more.

Write and let me know how long this letter takes to reach you. You'll have your hands full, I know, but being apart for a year does not mean we can't communicate. So I hope you'll write soon. And often.

After you get this adventure out of your system, we'll be ready to make solid plans for the future. You should have no trouble getting another teaching job, although that will seem mundane after living and teaching in the mountains of Nepal. We have a lot going for us. It will be time to move forward.

I'm looking forward to your first letter.

Yours,

Dan

Becca folded the letter and put it back in its envelope. Typical Dan: obviously he had things on his mind, but he could not come right out and say them. Somewhere between those lines lay a marriage proposal, in an indirect, assuming sort of way. He was so busy being efficient, he did not bother to say how he really felt.

"Good news?" Harriett was back.

"Any news from home is good news," Becca answered brightly.

"That's the way we all feel. It'll take longer for mail to reach you in the village, so cherish every piece."

"How much longer will it take? These took two weeks."

"There is delivery, but you can't always depend on it. The most reliable way is to wait until someone from the mission heads up your way. Usually the plane goes up there twice a week, but if they need the plane somewhere else, it won't go. We'll hold the letters here in the meantime."

Becca had not realized she would be cut off from her mail.

Harriett saw the disappointment in her face.

"It's hard," Harriett said. "I was in the Far West for a long time myself. But this way, when you get mail, you get a lot."

"I suppose so." Becca was not consoled.

"I came back out to ask if you are planning to be here for supper. I didn't see your name on the sign-up list."

"No, I won't be. Barnabas is coming to get me, and we're going to ride the bus to the market area. We thought we would get something to eat down there."

"You're going to ride the bus? Now there's a cultural experience for you."

Becca grimaced. "So I've heard. But it's part of the class. I'm going to have to do it without Barnabas by the end of the month."

Harriett smiled encouragingly. "Pay close attention today, then."

They heard a timid knock on the screen door. "There's Barnabas now," Becca said. "I guess I won't have time to change after all."

"Just wear comfortable shoes," Harriett advised.

❧

Becca and Barnabas set out on their expedition. They had to walk nearly a mile to the nearest intersection where a bus would pass. The dirt road that led to the mission guest house was much too narrow to accommodate the sort of bus they were looking for. Even without bus traffic, the street was overcrowded. Bicyclists and cars competed for the same limited space, tooting and honking at each other. No one ever stopped. To stop was to surrender your right to be on the road. Pedestrians walked boldly down the middle of the road, moving for cars only at the last minute and only if it was absolutely necessary. Becca, however, hugged the brick wall that lined the side of the street, wishing it were not even there so she could get farther away from the traffic. At one point, a cow settled down to rest in the middle of the road, causing a cacophony of objections from motorists. The cow swished her tail but did not move.

"I can't get used to the cows in the road," Becca said, raising her voice above the din in the street. "I know they are holy to the Hindus, but everyone seems annoyed with them."

"Yet they will do nothing about it," Barnabas said. "Even though they are bothersome, they are holy. Outside the city, it is not so much of a problem. There the cows have plenty of places to graze."

A taxi whizzed by closer than Becca liked, spewing out black exhaust. She covered her mouth and held her breath, but the dust stirred up by the car stung her eyes.

"I don't think I've seen a single traffic light since I got here," Becca said.

Barnabas smiled. "We have two. They just don't work. When the traffic is really bad, a policeman comes to the main intersections."

They reached the corner at last, and Becca breathed a sigh of relief at the sight of a sidewalk. Taking a walk in Porter was never this stressful. Unconsciously she had allowed her body to tense up, alert for the next onslaught of traffic. Now she could breathe freely for a few minutes.

It was not long before a bus thundered to the curb in front of them. Becca estimated that there were four people for every seat on the bus. Some did not even try to board; they simply gripped the molding on the rear of the bus. As the doors opened, Becca stepped back out of the way.

Barnabas nudged her forward. "This is our bus," he said.

"But it's full. Won't there be another one?"

"They are all like this. We must get on quickly." He pushed her forward into the crowd. She lunged up the steps just before the doors closed behind them.

Even in the clutches of a throng, Becca could see heads turning in her direction. What was an American woman doing, getting on a bus in Katmandu? she was sure they all wondered. She wondered herself. Becca did not know where to look, whether to meet their curious eyes or to ignore the stares. In fact, she did not have a choice. She had to put her face wherever there was a spot for it.

Unfortunately the place where it fit was directly behind the shoulder of someone who had not bathed recently. The whole bus smelled like a crowded workout room at the Porter Community Gym—only ten times worse. Becca was beginning to envy the people who were hanging out the windows. Even the polluted air of Katmandu was better than what she was breathing right then.

The bus lurched to a stop and Becca was thrown into the man in front of her. She tried to turn her head to find Barnabas, but she could not move. Four people squeezed down the aisle and exited the bus. To her horror, seven people got on. The bus belched and proceeded. Two more stops produced similar results. Each time she was pressed farther into the center aisle.

Just when Becca thought she was going to faint from lack of air, someone pulled at her elbow. She jumped and clutched her purse with both hands, wondering why she had brought a purse into such a circumstance.

"It's okay," a voice said. "It's me."

This time she persisted in her attempt to twist around to face Barnabas.

"The next stop is ours," he said.

"What a relief!" She followed his lead and inched her way toward the front of the bus. "How can you even see where we are?" she asked.

"I can't. I am counting the stops."

Becca tucked that hint away for future reference.

In another few minutes they were on the sidewalk again, breathing freely.

"Couldn't we have just taken a taxi?" Becca asked. "I would have been glad to pay."

Barnabas shook his head. "No, you must learn to do this. There may come a day when there is no taxi."

"But I'm going to a remote village. There won't be any buses there."

"Nor taxis," Barnabas reminded her. "Your options will be quite limited."

"I'll always have my feet."

"You will need them."

Becca scanned the area. Merchants spread their colorful wares on the sidewalk and sat and waited for customers. A woman crouched before an enormous loom and continued working on a half-finished rug. Pots, fabric, American clothing, furniture, traditional crafts—up and down the street, people were dickering over the asking price.

"Remember your assignment is to purchase something," Barnabas said. "It does not matter what it is as long as you practice the phrases you have been learning."

Becca nodded and let the phrases run through her head. She would give a traditional greeting of *Namaste* and then inquire about the cost of an item. She must not look too anxious to buy, or she would not be able to negotiate a lower price. Her eyes settled on a colorful cloth, something Karen would like.

"Are you ready?" Barnabas asked.

She nodded and thought, *Wait until you hear the story behind this one, Karen*. She took a deep breath and stepped toward the merchant.

six

Becca woke early. Behind the mission house, below her second-floor, rear window, was a row of lean-to houses. Patches of tin and aluminum, and sometimes just cardboard, were pressed into service to form walls and ceilings. Every piece was carefully counterbalanced to keep the shanties upright. Like a house of cards, pulling one piece would cause the collapse of several families' homes. Ragged lengths of cloth hung in the doorways, the only separation from the outside world. Windows were a luxury that none indulged in. Just outside the doorways, perhaps under a stretch of torn tarp, a fire might burn low to cook a pot of rice.

The alley community came to life as the sun came up. The sounds were muted at first, but as occupants awakened, the din multiplied and soaked up the brays of reluctant animals, the squeals of children who did not know they lived in poverty, the squawks of chickens doomed to be the day's dinner, the dinging bells on bicycles for those fortunate enough to have them. Voices rose and crisscrossed in the air, and the day was underway.

On her first morning in Nepal, Becca had been startled, nearly frightened, by the noise, and then appalled when she looked out her window and realized the source of it. That there was an entire community living in what amounted to a back alley outside the mission grounds was beyond anything she had imagined about Katmandu. Now, although she would have preferred to sleep a bit longer, she had grown used to the built-in alarm clock that beckoned her toward each day.

She still had more than three hours before she had to be in class. On most mornings, she used the time for studying. Only three days remained in her language program, and she was confident she had a good grasp of what she had been expected to learn in a month's time. She could relax and enjoy a morning of leisure. In a week's time she would be headed for her village, where she was sure she would be constantly occupied.

Becca was going to miss Katmandu. She had surprised herself by becoming attached to the dependable Harriett Metcalf and even stern and demanding Patricia Timbers. But the biggest surprise was her attachment to Barnabas. In the last two weeks, they had spent nearly every afternoon together. It began with assigned outings related to the culture portion of her course. They soon found that they were not in a hurry to get back to the mission house. Even when they made it back in time for dinner, Barnabas often stayed for an evening of conversation on the couch in the dining room, leaving only when Harriett threatened to throw him out so she could lock up for the night. Stuffing a pillow behind her back, Becca propped herself up as she reflected on the things they had done together.

Christians were not the only minority in the Hindu country of Nepal. There were also Buddhists, with their distinctive temples and visible Tibetan monks in traditional garb. Barnabas and Becca had climbed the steps of a well-known stupa and stood at the top, looking out over Katmandu. It was there that she had listened to Barnabas's vision for reaching his own people with the truth of Jesus; it was there she had glimpsed his passion for his life's work. It was more than work; it was a calling. Becca had become a teacher because she thought she would enjoy it; if she did not, she knew she could always try something else. Even in coming to Nepal, she convinced herself that she could turn back at any point. Not so for Barnabas. An outside force had grabbed hold of him, called him, convinced him that he could do nothing else than tell the story of Jesus. It was as if he had no choice but to obey. Without feeling self-conscious, he could stand atop a Buddhist or Hindu temple and pray for his people. And Becca, to her amazement, had joined him in lifting her hands and praying aloud, caught up in his passion and unmindful of any spectators. Never before had she met someone who had that effect on her, to find herself doing something she could not have imagined doing.

She had gone with Barnabas to his local church every Saturday since her arrival. While some of the other missionaries preferred the traditional Sunday observance and went to English-speaking churches, Becca tagged along with Barnabas. Sunday was a workday. The Nepali Christians met on Saturday, and she quickly fell into the rhythm. She had gone with an open mind and did not mind the lack of pews or the division between men and women. She simply removed her shoes at the door and went and sat among the other women on the dusty carpet, spread on the concrete floor. Barnabas moved to the front of the room and prepared to lead the singing.

Without Barnabas to translate, she could understand little of what was going on, especially at first. As the weeks progressed, she practiced her language with some brief conversations. But even without understanding the language, Becca repeatedly was struck by the beauty of the worship service. Here was a country where Christianity was virtually unknown fifty years earlier. They had not yet had time, generation upon generation, to become lethargic in their worship. When they prayed, they prayed aloud freely, their voices swelling as one toward heaven. When they sang, they sang heartily, not English hymns awkwardly translated into Nepali, but original, fresh Nepali songs. Barnabas and his team of musicians moved smoothly from one song to the next. Becca could hear his own sweet tenor voice as each new song began. She longed to be able to lift her own and join the harmony swirling around her. The tunes were easy. She learned them quickly and hummed when she did not know the words.

Becca and Barnabas had walked through the market streets

of Katmandu. The garment section was filled with tiny dark stalls with owners hawking their colorful saris and children's clothing. Others carried lengths of irresistible silk and printed cottons. A few blocks over, butchers hung their goat heads out and strung up pigs and chickens. On nearly every corner was a small Hindu shrine where the devout could stop to pray. Everywhere they walked, Barnabas grinned at people and struck up a conversation. Obviously he had walked the streets before; Becca was astonished by how many people recognized him and greeted him. His smile was genuine, as was his love for his people. People gladly accepted the literature he offered.

Yes, Becca concluded as she finally got out of bed, she would miss Barnabas more than she had bargained for at the start of her course.

The small desk was only a few steps from the bed. Becca picked up a half-finished letter she had started to Karen and scanned it.

Dear Karen,

I'm enclosing a few pictures of some scenes around Katmandu so you can see where I have been for the last four weeks. In some ways the whole setting is unreal to me—have I really come halfway around the world? So many things are different from what you and I are used to, from the food, to hot water (I've nearly forgotten what that is), to cows sleeping in the street next to parked motorcycles and rusty bikes. You would like the food; you've always had more tolerance than I have for hot seasonings. When I get home, I'll have to make you rice and curry the way they do it here.

Shopping is an experience out of this world. You can get a lot here in Katmandu, but you have to know where to go. I doubt that there is a Nepali word equivalent to "mall." Fortunately, I have a tutor who knows the city inside out, so he has been a great help.

Becca stared at the words on the page. She was talking through the mail, telling Karen all the trivial details that they would share in person. But she had confined herself to the trivialities. Her words did not begin to tell Karen what her experience of Nepal was really like—or the significance of meeting someone like Barnabas. For the first time in their seven-year friendship, Becca was holding back from Karen.

Would Karen even understand the kind of conviction and passion of Barnabas? Had she ever felt so moved by something? Did her work as an editor drive her the way Barnabas's work propelled him toward his dream? And would Karen understand if Becca admitted her feelings about Barnabas, feelings that she did not understand herself. She was supposed to be in love with Dan Stockwell back in Porter; they were practically engaged. That is what she told herself. But being with Barnabas cast doubt on her relationship with Dan. From a distance of twelve time zones, it was easy to wonder what was real back home, what was genuine, and what was simply assumed.

Becca sat down on the bed again and debated her choices. She could finish the chatty letter to Karen, and her friend would never know the difference. Or she could take a new path and tell the truth. She picked up her pen and started writing.

My tutor's name is Barnabas, and he is the first Nepali Christian that I've met. He is a leader in one of the largest churches in Katmandu and works for an organization that produces Christian literature and tapes. He wants to learn to be a pilot so he can fly to the remote parts of the country—places where there are no roads. His family is Hindu and while they want him to be a pilot, they are pressuring him to marry a Hindu woman before he goes for training.

Karen, Barnabas is one of the most impressive people I've ever met. I never expected to form this kind of attachment to a language tutor. But he has been so much more than that. He has become a good friend. My only regret about leaving Katmandu at this point in time is that I have to leave him behind. I'm really going to miss him. It never occurred to me that I might feel such fondness for a Nepali man. After all, there's Dan, waiting for me. But I do feel something, and I think Barnabas does, too.

There. She had said it. But there was more.

The admiration and respect that I feel for Barnabas has made me reevaluate a lot of things in my life, including my relationship with Dan. I know you won't betray any secrets to him, so it is safe for me to say that I am drawn to Barnabas because of qualities he has that Dan does not have. And that makes me question why Dan and I have been together. Now I can see that we needed this time away from each other.

In a few more days I move to the village, so the next letter will come from there. It may be a while; the mail is slow. But know that I am thinking of you every day, my friend.

Love,

Becca

Becca licked the envelope, sealed it, and addressed it. Barnabas had taken her to the post office once before; she would ask him to go one more time. She was certain they would want to spend the afternoon together anyway. This time he would insist that she negotiate the way through Katmandu, while he playfully provided security lest she make a wrong turn. Setting the letter on top of her textbook, she started dressing and getting ready to go down for breakfast.

There was so much more Becca had not told Karen. As much as she was drawn to Barnabas, she was also frightened by her feelings. If she were right, and Barnabas was fond of her, too, what would it mean for the future? Was she prepared to consider staying in Nepal more than one year? Although Barnabas wanted to go to the States to study, he did not want to stay there. She chided herself for jumping ahead of the circumstances. So much remained unspoken between them. The longer she was in Nepal, the more she realized that she had much more to learn about herself, apart from other relationships.

And what about Dan? Was she being fair to him? She was comfortable with Dan and fond of him, but she was neither inspired nor excited by him. Did she need to be challenged in order to love? She struggled with whether she should expect to be provoked by a man or whether she should find her own confrontations within herself. Either choice might mean leaving Dan behind. Was she prepared to do that, after everything she had invested in their relationship?

Becca ran her hands through her frizzy hair. Every day her feelings grew more complicated. The clock told her that it was time to get serious about getting ready for breakfast. She reached for her brush. She would have to ponder the complexities of her life later. Barnabas would be waiting for her in the classroom.

seven

On her way through the dining room, Becca drank a glass of watery powdered milk, wishing it were real orange juice, and spread some jelly on a piece of bread. Breakfast was not on her mind. She was sure Barnabas would be at the school already, and if she went early, they would have a chance to talk before class.

She walked confidently through the streets of Katmandu to the school, about half a mile from the mission compound. A month earlier she would not have stepped outside the gate without a companion. Now she slung her backpack over her shoulder, lengthened her gait, and strode purposefully toward the school, munching on her bread as she walked. Heads still turned and looked at the young American woman alone in the street, but she no longer minded. Why shouldn't they be curious about her? She was curious about them.

At the school, she looked for Barnabas in the dining room and several classrooms. She even ventured to try out her Nepali and asked the cook if he had seen Barnabas. He was nowhere to be found. Becca thought it odd that he should change his habit at this point in the course; perhaps he would be along soon.

She settled on an outside step where she could enjoy the morning sun and she unzipped her backpack. The idle moments could be profitably spent writing a letter to her parents. She had not sent Dan more than a short note so far, and now she did not know what she would say to him when she did write. Writing her parents was less complicated, so she settled in for the task.

Before long, others began to arrive: the European businessmen, then Patricia, then the American doctor. The tutors straggled in, one at a time. But not Barnabas. It was time to start class, and he still was not there. Her concern growing, Becca dragged herself up the wooden stairs and tried to concentrate on what Patricia was saying.

"You've come a long way in four weeks," Patricia said. "One or two of you have a real knack for language work and will be fluent very soon. It will take longer for others, but it is satisfying to see that you have all met the requirements of the course. Your tutors tell me that you are ready to be turned loose, but I'm not going to let you off the hook yet. We have a few more details to work on in these last three days."

As she glanced around the room, Becca recalled her doubts on the first day of class. The high ceiling, the decorative walls, the dim lights, the rickety chairs—despite these things, this room had been a place of learning. Patricia Timbers, with far less than ideal conditions, had done her job as a teacher, and Becca's respect for her had grown. She hoped she would do as well when facing an improvised classroom in the village. She would remember this place with inspiration.

Becca looked over at the chair where Barnabas usually sat. It was empty. Much of her success was because of his skill and patience as a tutor. She could not imagine having gone through the course without him. Today, when the time came for individual work with tutors, Patricia sat and worked with Becca on some unusual verb forms.

"Did Barnabas tell you he was not coming?" Becca asked Patricia.

"No, I thought perhaps you knew where he was," Patricia answered. Clearly she had observed the growing friendship between student and tutor. They both shrugged their shoulders and turned back to the textbook.

Late in the morning, when they were once again working as a large group, Barnabas slipped into the room. Becca heard his chair creak and looked over at him and smiled. He returned the gesture with half of his mouth, but his eyes were gloomy. The smile was not coming from inside him. He had a piece of paper in front of him and looked at it repeatedly, rather than paying attention to what Patricia was saying.

Becca was no longer paying attention to Patricia, either. *I know so little about him*, she thought, with sudden realization. *I have no idea where he might have been this morning*. Barnabas took his responsibilities seriously, she knew that. What could have happened to keep him away? For weeks he had been consistently serene, unruffled by the dilemma he faced. What had changed? She had never seen him looking so distressed, but she had known him for only a month. There could be a dozen explanations. Perhaps his calm exterior was not so constant as she had assumed.

At last the lunch break came. Becca assumed Barnabas would walk down to the dining room with her, as was their habit. Sometimes they ate with other students, but often they sat alone and conversed freely on a personal level. Today, however, he darted out of the room before she got to the door. She saw his dark head bobbing down the stairs and she stifled the urge to call out to him. The stone in her stomach told her that whatever was going on was serious.

Becca, absorbed in thought, trailed behind the others down the stairs and along the path to the dining room. As she crossed the courtyard, she saw Barnabas. Her steps slowed even more, wondering if she could catch his eye. He was talking intently with another man she did not recognize. Barnabas's face was grim and pale. At one point, he dragged his toe through the dirt, his head hanging low. He seemed not to notice Becca.

Increasingly concerned but helpless to take any action, she got her food and considered where to sit. The table where she often sat with Barnabas was vacant, and she was tempted to sit there and wait for him, but the American doctor caught her eye.

"Come sit with us, Becca," he said. "Looks like your friend is tied up."

Apparently the whole class had drawn their conclusions about her relationship with Barnabas. She could hardly blame them. She and Barnabas had been quite overt, particularly in the last week or so.

Becca smiled at the doctor and accepted his invitation to sit down. She had no assurance that Barnabas would come in at all. She might as well sit and eat her lunch. Politely she listened as the others talked about their assignments and where they would be going in the next few days.

"How are you getting to your village?" someone asked.

"One of the fathers of the children I'll be teaching is coming to escort me," she answered.

"Will you be flying?"

"I hope so," she answered nervously. "There aren't many seats available on those small planes, and they go only twice a week at most."

"Don't you have a reservation?"

"Not yet. Apparently they do not consider me a priority."

"What are your alternatives?"

"They tell me that the only other way to get there is a sixteen-hour bus ride followed by a four-day hike up the mountain."

"I'd hold out for the plane."

Becca nodded. That was her intention.

The conversation drifted to the travel plans of others in the group and Becca listened half-heartedly. As she ate, periodically she glanced up casually to look at Barnabas and the strange man. The man gestured expressively and energetically; Barnabas looked grief-stricken.

"We're going to take a quick walk to the shops up the street," the doctor said, interrupting Becca's analysis. "Do you want to come?"

"No thanks. I think I'll just have some tea and let my food settle." The group left, and she was grateful for the solitude. Now she could watch Barnabas without inhibition. He did not look any less distressed.

As Becca swallowed the last of her rice, Barnabas and the stranger finally entered the dining room and came and sat across from her.

"Good afternoon, Rebecca," Barnabas said. The tension in his voice was an unfamiliar tone.

"Good afternoon," she answered. She wanted to say so much more. She looked from Barnabas to the man and tried to smile. "Are you going to eat?"

He shook his head. "Rebecca, I would like you to meet my Uncle Krishna. He is my mother's oldest brother."

"I am very glad to meet you," she said sincerely. She had been curious about Barnabas's family.

"It is my pleasure," Krishna said graciously. "My nephew has told me that you are his student. I hope he has given satisfactory service as a tutor."

"Oh, more than satisfactory. He has been more helpful than I ever imagined."

"He is a man of many talents. And many dreams."

"Yes," Becca agreed, wondering if Barnabas and his uncle had been discussing those dreams.

"My nephew says you are a Christian, like he is," Krishna said.

"Yes, I am. That is another reason why it has been good to know Barnabas."

"Ah, yes, that is his Christian name. I am not used to using it."

"Oh, I didn't realize—"

"I was given a Hindu name when I was born," Barnabas said softly. "But I have chosen a Christian name for myself."

"I see."

"I know some other Christians in Pokhara, where I live," Krishna said. "They are very nice people. They have some strange ideas, but they have been very kind to me."

Becca did not know what to say. Krishna delivered her from the moment of awkwardness by standing up to leave.

"I must take my leave. I am very glad to have met you." He

bowed toward her graciously.

"And I am glad to meet you, also," Becca responded. "Perhaps I will see you again."

After Krishna had left the room and was well across the courtyard, Becca turned to Barnabas, her eyes searching for an explanation in his.

"Krishna has brought news from my parents," Barnabas began. "A letter."

"Bad news?"

"They do not think so. They have settled on a wife for me. They want me to come home to Pokhara and get married."

"When?" Becca asked in alarm.

"In three months. As a wedding gift, my father will give me the money that I need to become a pilot in the U.S."

"This is an impossible situation," Becca said plainly.

"Quite so. I wish to respect my parents' wishes. I believe God wants me to honor my parents. But I believe He would want me to marry a Christian woman and raise a Christian family. I cannot marry this woman."

"Barnabas, I don't know what to say."

He shook his head. "No, it would be difficult for you to understand. In your culture young people are free to make their own decisions. They are encouraged to leave their parents' homes and choose for themselves. But in our country these things are not left to the young. The elders have authority and we must respect them."

"Can you talk to your parents and ask for more time?"

"I have done that over and over. It was my hope that I would find a Christian woman to marry. Perhaps if they found her acceptable in all respects except her religion, they would relent. If they knew that I cared for someone, I do not think they would make me go against my heart. I have asked God many times to show me who will be my wife. And now it is time for me to get married. They have been very patient to wait this long."

Becca chose her words carefully. "But you haven't met anyone?"

"No one that I have been sure of. Recently, perhaps, I have met someone. God has not yet given me a sign. And I do not know if my parents would accept her." Barnabas met Becca's gaze. "She is an American."

Becca caught her breath. "Barnabas, I didn't know—"

"We have not spoken of such things. And perhaps we should not speak of them now. If I had not received this letter, I would not be so bold."

Becca wanted to ask him to speak his mind more directly, but she knew this was no moment to appear like a pushy American.

Barnabas fumbled awkwardly with a loose button on his sweater. "I am sorry, Rebecca. I have no place to speak to you in this fashion. Please forgive me."

"There is nothing to forgive, Barnabas. I think we have become good friends. I am flattered that you can speak freely to me." Inside, she was screaming, *I feel the same way! Don't marry the woman your parents have chosen. It's too soon!*

"You are easy to talk to. I cannot talk the same way to a woman from my country. I hope you will pray for me. This is a difficult choice."

"Of course I will."

"If I marry, I can go to the U.S. I can learn to be a pilot, and I will be one step closer to what God has called me to do."

Becca nodded in agreement, not speaking the counter argument.

"But how can I serve God as an evangelist if I am married to a Hindu? This is impossible."

"Perhaps she will come to faith," Becca ventured, allowing for the possibility that Barnabas would indeed be backed into the corner and marry the woman his parents had chosen.

"Of course that would be my hope and prayer. But Hinduism

runs very deeply in Nepal. It is very difficult to separate the culture from the religion. And I would not want her to change her religion to please me if she did not truly believe."

"This is very complicated." Becca sighed deeply. "There is no easy answer."

"No. . .no. If only. . ."

She knew his thoughts had returned to the idea that if he had found a wife on his own, even a Christian, his parents might not pressure him into a Hindu marriage. And, given time, perhaps their relationship would be one that he could tell his parents about. But they did not have time. He had only three months, perhaps less, before he would have to commit himself or dishonor his parents by refusing their wishes.

If Becca revealed her feelings of fondness for Barnabas now, she risked misleading him. She was uncertain of her own feelings. She knew she would have to resolve things with Dan before she could move on to a new commitment. And the possibility of marriage to a Nepali was overwhelming, with implications for the rest of her life.

As Becca met Barnabas's eyes, a tear slipped from her own.

eight

The butterflies flapped and fluttered, struggling to be free. They beat their wings in vain for they could move only from one side of their prison to the other. Becca put her hand on her stomach to try to quell the movement, but her gesture had no effect. She was nervous, more nervous than she had thought she would be at the point of her departure. The mission guest house had offered her safe refuge for the last month, a place to come home to at the end of each day and collect her thoughts and emotions. In a matter of minutes, she would be leaving this place for yet another unknown.

She could not help but long for something familiar: a phone conversation with Karen, a date with Dan, something predictable. Instead, she sat on the couch in the dining room of the guest house and kept an ear cocked for the taxi that would soon arrive to take her to the airport. The missionary who had come to Katmandu to escort her was taking advantage of his trip to do some shopping for his family; he was due back with the taxi at any moment, and together they would go on to the airport.

To herself, Becca also had to admit that she was waiting to see if Barnabas would come to say goodbye. They had been together two days ago when word arrived that at last she had been assigned a seat on the small plane that would take her to her village. She had expected to wait several more days, but Barnabas had not been surprised.

"God wants you to go to the village," he said confidently. "Finding you a seat on the plane is a small thing."

"From the point of view of theology, I have to agree," she had responded. "But from the point of view of practical experience, things don't always work out so easily."

Barnabas had fallen into silence. After a moment, he spoke quietly. "God will solve my problem, too."

"Of course, He will." Becca spoke words of agreement, but in her heart, she was not so sure. Barnabas's problem was so much bigger than her own. Getting a seat on the plane was only a matter of time and waiting another few days would have had no lasting consequences. But if Barnabas were pressured into marrying a Hindu woman. . . Becca hated to think what that would mean for his future. Somehow he had regained his calm since his uncle's visit. He had not again displayed the torture of that day.

The sound of a motor startled her, even though she was waiting for one. She turned her head to look out the window and saw not a taxi but a motorcycle. Barnabas unfastened his helmet and grinned at her as he removed it. Becca got up and pushed open the door.

"I didn't think you were coming," she said. "You must have a hundred things you need to do today."

"I admit that I cannot stay long," he said. "But it seems fitting that I should see you off." He leaned back against his bike, still smiling.

"You sure look happy today," she said.

"The Lord is good. Why should I not be happy?"

Once again, Becca was filled with admiration for Barnabas. He truly believed all the things she had grown up reciting in church.

"What will you do now that the course is over?" she asked.

"Ah, I have many things. I will go to visit several villages quite soon and take some tapes to them. And we are working on some tracts. I must have them ready for the printer soon. Another course begins in a few weeks."

He would be busy, Becca concluded. Would he miss her as much as she would miss him? "Thank you for everything you have done for me," she said. "I don't know how I could have gotten through the course without you."

"You worked very hard."

She wanted to ask, *When will I see you again?* Instead, she said, "They tell me I can come back to Katmandu for a couple of weeks halfway through my year."

"I will try to be here."

She nodded, not able to say more.

Another motor filled the courtyard; the taxi had arrived. The missionary emerged from the back seat. "Barnabas! What are you doing here?" said David Bridgman.

"I have come to say goodbye to my favorite student."

"You were Becca's tutor?"

Barnabas nodded and grinned. "I am glad to see she is going to be in good hands."

Becca looked on as Barnabas and David continued with their reunion. She had not realized that they knew each other. The taxi driver stood by, looking impatient.

"Are your things ready?" David asked Becca.

"Just inside the door." Becca slung one bag over her shoulder and let the three men load the others into the small trunk.

David clasped Barnabas's hand energetically and said, "Maybe the next time I come through we can spend some time together."

"I would like that." He turned to Becca. "You will be happy with the Bridgmans. They will look after you well."

Becca nodded and forced a smile.

"Better get going," David said, opening a door for Becca. Before Becca knew it, the taxi had pulled out of the courtyard and Barnabas was lost from her eyes.

As they pulled into traffic at the main intersection, David Bridgman launched into explanations. "I've been so busy shopping and trying to get the things we need that we haven't spent any time talking about the village. I don't know how much the agency has told you."

"Only that there are five families and eleven children of school age, ranging from six to thirteen years old."

"That's right. Altogether, we have sixteen children, but some are still young. Not everyone lives right in the village, but we use that as a base largely so that the children can be schooled together. The mission has been generous in providing a teacher."

"How long have you been there?"

"Eight years. I'm an agriculturalist. I'm sure you know that no one comes into Nepal with a visa that screams that they are a missionary. Everyone has an occupation that the government thinks will make a contribution to the development of Nepal."

"How many children do you and your wife have?"

"Three. Jill is thirteen, Mandy is seven, and Jake is four." David tilted his head thoughtfully "We're not sure how much longer we can keep Jill with us. She really needs to come to Katmandu for a proper high school education. She hasn't quite adjusted since we got back from furlough about six months ago."

They arrived at the airport. David checked them in and made sure her luggage was loaded. Hesitantly, Becca climbed into the small craft. She could not even stand up straight. She was reminded of newspaper stories of small aircraft hitting a rough wind and whirling to the ground. Would this small plane be able to rise above the grand Himalayas? There were two pilot seats and five passenger seats. With her stomach in her throat, she sat very still in her seat while the plane taxied and lifted off. David chattered intermittently during the two-hour flight, obviously accustomed to this mode of transportation. Becca hardly heard anything he said but nodded at polite intervals.

When Becca finally allowed herself to lean over and look out the window, the view astounded her. Outside Katmandu proper, lush fields rolled into hillsides and up the walls of the valley. From the air she could see that Katmandu was set strategically in a basin, surrounded by mountains on all sides. But the city was creeping out in every direction and soon the valley would be consumed.

From the air Becca got her first real look at the famed Himalayas, which had not been visible from the valley. Only the work of skilled photographers had prepared her for their beauty. She felt her eyes widen and her jaw drop. For a moment, their beauty absorbed her fears.

At last the descent began. Becca truly began to relax; it would be good to be on solid ground again, even in unfamiliar territory. She breathed a sigh of relief when the wheels touched the ground and the plane came to rest in a grassy opening in a level spot on the hillside.

"Take a look out the window," David said, "and see the hike you would have had to take if there had been no plane."

Becca looked. They were well up the side of the mountain. Despite long walks with Barnabas during the afternoons of the last month, she doubted that she was in physical condition to make the climb and uttered a prayer of thanks for the plane, as doubtful as she had been.

"Ready?" David asked. "We're the only ones getting off here."

Moments later, Becca stood at the end of the short runway and watched the plane lift off again. Her last connection to life as she knew it was fading from sight, boring into the western sun. *What have I gotten myself into?* she wondered. *I don't know what I'm doing here!*

"Let me introduce you to everybody," David said, touching her elbow to point her toward the village. "We'll still have to walk a bit. The porters will bring your things."

Becca nodded and followed David; she did not know what else to do.

They walked for about two miles. The grassy opening gave way to a forested incline; the path through the trees was well-worn and reasonably wide. The angle of the mountain was fairly steep, though, and the muscles in Becca's calves soon protested what was being asked of them. She felt sorry for the small, wiry men serving as her porters but comforted herself with the knowledge that they were in much better physical condition than she was. Gradually, small buildings began showing up along the widening dirt path, and a village emerged.

It was a good-sized village, larger than Becca had visualized. The road widened into an intersection and the village sprawled out from that center. Small wooden buildings lined the streets. At one corner of town, women scrubbed clothes against rocks in a stream and hung them out to dry. Across the way was a collection of garden patches sprouting vegetables.

"How many people live here?" Becca asked incredulously.

"About four thousand," David answered. "A lot of them are just scraping by with their vegetable plots. The soil up here is pretty rocky, but with enough care, things can grow."

"It's beautiful!"

"It is scenic, I'll grant you that. But it is also rustic. Remember, there is no electricity or running water up here. We do things the hard way."

"Yes, I was expecting that. They said there was a generator?"

"We do have a generator, but we run it only in the evening. Otherwise we depend on the sun." David laughed softly. "You'll find yourself doing a lot of things outside."

Becca looked up and down the street. "There are so many children," she commented. Most of them needed a bath but probably did not know it.

"We've been trying to get a Sunday school going. We teach our own children, of course, and the children of the few Christians that live up here. But we want to teach the villagers. Many of the parents are very skeptical, still. They work beside us all week on agricultural or low-technology engineering projects, but they don't quite trust us when it comes to sending their kids to Sunday school, which actually meets on Saturday."

Becca caught the eyes of a child and smiled into their blackness. Reluctantly, the little girl smiled back, twirling the hem of her faded dress.

"What about regular school for them? Is there one?"

David shrugged. "Some of the older boys go in the mornings. But most of them are needed by their families."

"What about the girls?"

David shook his head sadly. "Educating a girl is not important to the villagers. You must have read something in your culture course about the low role of women here."

Becca nodded. She had indeed learned that Nepali women had a hard life, and that few outside the city ever learned to read. And now she was seeing the textbook facts come to life.

David gestured toward a solid-looking house, larger than most of the rest. "Here we are. This is my home."

They entered the front door and were met by four pairs of eyes. "This is Sandy, my wife, and our children, Jill, Mandy, and Jake."

"I'm glad to meet all of you," Becca said. Jake disappeared behind his mother's legs.

"Say hello to Miss Masterson," Sandy Bridgman instructed her children.

"Please, call me Rebecca. Or just Becca."

"I'm not going to call her anything, 'cause I'm not going to school," seven-year-old Mandy announced.

"We've been having a few discussions lately," Sandy said apologetically. "It's been several weeks since the last teacher left, and Mandy has decided that she would rather work or play with the village children than go to school."

"There ought to be time for both," Becca assured Mandy.

Sandy gestured toward her older daughter. "Jill is the only one her age, but she's a strong, independent student. Just get her started on something, and she'll catch on quickly."

Becca smiled at Jill, who still had not spoken. She remembered that David had said she was not adjusting to their return to the village. "What have you been studying lately?" Becca asked.

Jill shrugged. "Just regular stuff."

"Well, I think we can do better than that. We'll have to talk more about what you're interested in."

"Whatever."

"Jill," Sandy said, warning her with her tone.

"I'm sorry," the girl muttered.

"Why don't we take a look at the classroom. Then you can get settled in." Sandy led the way through the house to a spacious and airy back porch.

"We've talked for years about constructing a separate building just for the school," David explained. "Somehow it just never gets done."

"This almost feels like being outside," Becca commented. "That's the next best thing to not having to go to school at all." She winked at Mandy.

The screened-in porch held an assortment of student desks, a large metal teacher's desk, and two bookshelves. The one solid wall bore a chalkboard and a bulletin board. Becca glanced at the world map taped to the wall; it did not show the many changes in country names and borders of the last few years. A closer inspection of the bookshelves revealed a fair selection of textbooks for various ages, but not much supplementary reading material.

As if reading Becca's thoughts, Sandy said, "We've asked the mission and the churches back home for more books. Just storybooks, or books that are interesting to look at. We're promised that they are coming."

"Perhaps one of them will be an atlas," Becca said hopefully. "I've brought a few things along with me. We'll have to get creative, but we'll manage." She put as much hope into her tone as she could but as she surveyed the classroom again and the faces of Mandy and Jill, Becca knew she had a lot of work ahead of her.

nine

The weeks flew. Becca started classes immediately and sandwiched in the tasks of taking an inventory of available books and supplies, rearranging the furniture, and making lesson plans for students at five different grade levels. After two weeks, Mandy Bridgman was still hollering about having to go to school, but while she was there she worked hard. Becca devised trips into the forest with science mysteries for the children to solve. Mandy began to come around and after four weeks, she was the first one to arrive in the morning.

Most of the other children were cooperative about studying. Files from the regular teacher, who would be returning after a year's furlough, told Becca the strengths and areas of need for each child and she was able to make individual plans for what she hoped to accomplish with each student during the year. Tommy needed to work on reading comprehension; Matthew was talented at mathematics and was ready for algebra; Hannah was a gifted writer but shy about demonstrating her ability. All of the younger children warmed up to their new teacher.

Jill remained aloof. Although she completed her assignments on time, she rarely spoke during the day, and Becca could not remember seeing her smile. With the other children, Becca rose to the challenge of being a teacher in the truest sense—not dependent on curriculum or textbooks, but building on natural interests and abilities. She was exhilarated and was stretched far beyond teaching a stable group of third graders in the United States. Jill seemed out of reach, but Becca was determined to penetrate the wall that the adolescent had constructed around herself.

About two weeks into her crusade, during the course of an ordinary assignment, Becca discovered that Jill had read several of John Steinbeck's novels, and the two of them had a lively discourse on their favorite passages. Becca racked her brain to remember what other novels she had seen in the bookcase at the mission guest house. Surely there would be a way to get some of those for Jill to read.

A week later, Becca had been out for a walk in the late afternoon and had come across Jill, leaning against a tree and writing in a diary. At first she had been reluctant to disturb Jill and so she widened her route to circle around the girl. But Jill saw her and caught her eye.

"Isn't it spectacular?" Jill said, looking at the mountainside view.

Becca accepted this indirect invitation for conversation and sat on the ground next to Jill. Becca expected Jill to cut short their visit at any moment, but they talked until suppertime. After that, Becca was alert for any opportunity to extend friendship to her lone adolescent student.

At the end of her fourth week, Becca sat at the used, metal desk and began reading the compositions the children had turned in that day. She decided to start with papers from the younger children and work her way up. Concentrating on deciphering Mandy's second-grade scrawl, Becca hardly heard the footsteps or the door creak open. She happened to glance up and saw Jill, rummaging quietly through a desk.

"Hi, Jill," Becca said brightly. "Forget something?"

The girl nodded. "My geometry book. I'm supposed to do five problems before tomorrow."

"Ah, yes. Is it there in the desk?"

Jill pulled it out and held it up wordlessly. She started to leave.

Becca got up and quickly stepped toward Jill. "You're doing very well with your geometry. You must like it."

Jill shrugged. "It's all right."

"Tell me, Jill, what do you like? Your sister has enjoyed the special science projects. There's no reason why we couldn't do something like that for you. Not everything you learn has to come from a book."

"It doesn't really matter."

Becca perched on a desk and looked Jill in the eye. "I think it does matter. Usually students who do as well as you do, really like school. You get nearly perfect marks, and I know you like to read. But it's clear you are not enjoying school."

Jill did not respond. She just looked away from Becca and stared at a spot on the floor.

"Has school always been this way for you?" Becca probed, hoping to sound less like a teacher and more like a friend.

"I used to like it," the girl admitted. "Last year, I really liked it."

"Why did you like it so well? Do you miss your regular teacher?"

"No, you're a good teacher. But last year I went to a real school."

"A real school?"

"In Kansas."

"Oh, yes, your family was in the States for furlough, right?"

Jill nodded.

"And you enjoyed it?"

Jill looked as if she was struggling with a response. Finally, she said, "Not at first. I didn't remember much about the last furlough, and I didn't want to go. And then, when I got there, I didn't have any friends."

"But that changed?"

"I went to a great school and made a lot of friends. It was hard to come back."

"Don't you feel you belong here, with your family?"

"I suppose so."

"You don't sound too sure."

"I don't really fit anywhere. I don't belong in the States anymore. I'm different from those kids. But I don't belong here, either." The truth was out; this was the core of Jill's problem. Now that she had admitted it, the gates opened wide.

"You're just here for a year," Jill said, her voice cracking. "You get to go back. There's no big decision to make. You'll fit in when you go back. But I don't fit."

Becca chose her words carefully. She did not want to waste the rare opportunity with Jill. "Being in Nepal has already changed me. It's not the same as growing up here, like you have, but being in another culture for even a couple of months makes me appreciate people like your parents. They sacrifice comfortable lives to do something they really believe in. I'm not sure I could do that."

"That was their choice," countered Jill. "I'm just along for the ride."

"What do you mean?"

"I didn't choose to live in Nepal. What if I would rather be in America?"

"Would you?" Becca pressed.

"Maybe. I don't know. I just know my life doesn't make any sense, all scrambled up like this."

"You know what?"

"What?" Jill tentatively lifted her eyes to Becca's.

"My life is scrambled up, too."

"It is?"

"Sure. Some days I wake up and wish I were home in Ohio and could go out to my favorite restaurant for a great meal. Or I wish I could just lie in a hammock on a summer afternoon, reading a novel. Or I wish I were back with my class of third graders where I knew exactly what I was doing."

"But you will be."

Becca nodded. "If I want to, I probably can go back to my job. But I'm not sure I'll want to. Teaching you all here has been more of a challenge than anything I've done back home. I feel like I'm doing something really valuable, something that matters."

"You're doing something that matters, but you're not sacrificing your whole life, like my parents have."

"I admire your parents, Jill."

"I know, I know." Jill was on the verge of groaning. "They're missionaries, and everyone is in awe of missionaries. But look at what you're doing. You came all the way over here to be a teacher for one year. That's important, too. And it proves that it is possible to do something important without giving up your whole life."

"Everything we do changes us in some way." Becca paused. "I know I'll be different when I go back, but I don't know how different."

"But at least it's something that you chose. You can do what you want."

"Do you really wish you were back in the States, going to a regular school?"

"I don't know. I just want to do something because I chose it, not because my parents are missionaries."

"I can understand that."

"No one else seems to. I'm too young to decide anything for myself."

"Maybe, maybe not."

Jill looked up, questioning.

Becca continued. "I'll admit, there are some things that your parents should decide for you, until you're a little older. But that doesn't mean you can't choose to make a difference for somebody."

"But how? I'm just a kid."

"Take stock of your abilities. What are you good at?"

"Well. . .I'm a good student. I take care of my brother and sister."

"That's great. What else?"

"I think that someday. . .I might like. . ."

"What is it, Jill? You can tell me."

"I'd like to be a teacher."

Becca started to smile. "Jill, there's one more thing. How many languages do you speak?"

"Besides English?"

"Yes, besides English."

"Just Nepali."

"What do you mean, 'just Nepali'?" Becca chided. "How many kids at that great school in the U.S. can speak Nepali?"

"I never thought much about it. I learned it when I was really little. It was just part of growing up here."

"But you can do something I can't do. Oh, I studied Nepali for a few weeks, but I'm nowhere near being fluent, like you are."

"But. . .I don't get it."

"Jill, I've been wanting to teach some of the little Nepali girls how to read. I know a lot of them will never get the chance to go to a real school. But I can't do it because I'm just learning their language. But you could do it."

Jill's eyes widened. "Do you really think so?"

"Of course I do. I'd be happy to help as much as I can, but you would have to be the teacher."

And so, Jill and Becca spent the rest of the afternoon making plans. They would start with a small group of girls, perhaps older girls who had not been able to go to school. Then the older ones could teach the younger ones. It might be difficult to find some time each day when the girls could get away from their chores, but Jill had some ideas, and Becca decided to leave the organization of the project to her excited partner. She could stand back, staying near enough to come to Jill's help when needed but far enough to let Jill feel that the project was her own. As a language arts project over the next two weeks, Jill would create a set of primer books that used only a few words and talked about ordinary village activities. Then they would begin in earnest.

"It's almost time for supper," Jill said after nearly two hours. "You're eating with us tonight, aren't you?"

"That's right. Two more nights with you, then on to the next family."

Becca took her meals with the missionary families on a rotating basis. The families all had household help for preparing meals. At first Becca felt awkward and thought she would rather fix her own food. But the reality was that food preparation was much more time consuming than at home in Porter, and she had not come halfway around the world to spend several hours a day scrubbing vegetables and boiling drinking water. So she relented and ate with the missionaries.

That night at supper Becca squeezed in around the Bridgman table and watched Jill's glowing eyes as she described the idea for her parents.

❧

After supper each night, Becca would retire to her own tiny, two-room house. She had a small bedroom and a second room that she used for reading and studying. Both rooms together were not as big as the living room in her apartment in Porter, but Becca had long ago stopped noticing.

After her long, unexpected discussion with Jill, Becca had a hard time concentrating on her work. She still wanted to grade the compositions that she had started earlier in the day. When she got to her house after supper, she checked her watch and saw that she would have less than an hour of generator power. When the generator was turned off for the night, her light would go out. She shuffled the papers, hoping to find one that was particularly interesting to start out with.

As she scanned the paragraphs and made routine corrections on grammar and spelling, Becca's mind was on something else.

She was pleased to have finally connected with Jill and excited about what they could accomplish together. But the young girl had brought to the surface questions rankling in Becca's mind as well. She had been gone from the U.S. for only two months; she knew that she had not yet made any substantial sacrifice. Although living conditions were tedious in the village, Jill was right when she pointed out that Becca could go home. She had come looking for adventure, and she had found it. She could satisfy that urge, do the job she came to do—and do it well—then go home to a spacious apartment and a well-equipped classroom. No, she had not sacrificed anything.

When she had left Porter, Becca had assumed that she would return after one year and finally marry Dan Stockwell. Now she was not sure about anything. Would she still want to marry Dan? Would she even want to be in Porter? If she were honest with herself, she had to admit that she missed Barnabas and Katmandu more than she missed Dan and Porter. What was she to make of that surprise? Could she, in her wildest imagination, consider not going home at the end of her year of teaching in the village?

Becca heard the familiar groan of the generator just before the lights cut out. With a familiar movement, she reached for the matches and lit a candle.

Her intention was to finish marking the papers by the light of the candle. Instead, she stared into the flickering flame, watching it twist and swirl. The candle burned slowly, and she lost track of time. Finally, she blew it out and slipped into bed, her questions still hanging in the dark.

ten

The last of the missionary children was out the door at last, joyously released into the hands of their Nepali companions for the rest of the afternoon. When the porch door had swung closed, Becca let herself sag into the chair behind her desk. Her job amounted to teaching five different grades at one time, none of them third grade, the level she was most used to. She scrambled to stay two steps ahead of the children and be prepared for each day's tasks.

After one last longing look at the sunshine outside, Becca flipped open her black, lesson plan book and started sketching out what she would try to accomplish the next week. In her concentration, she almost did not hear the soft knock on the porch door. Without looking up, she said absently, "Yes?" She expected it to be one of the little Nepali girls Jill was teaching to read.

"If I am disturbing you, I can come back later."

Becca's eyes flew up. That voice—it was Barnabas!

She stood up and rushed toward him. "What are you doing here?" she asked.

Without thinking, she threw her arms around him. Only when Barnabas returned the embrace did it occur to Becca that they had never hugged each other before, not even when she had left Katmandu.

"I was in a nearby village," Barnabas explained. "How could I come so near and not see you? So I have come."

"I'm so glad you did. Can you stay long? Will we have a chance to talk?" Becca stepped back to her desk and pulled her chair around for him to sit on. She perched on a small desk across from him.

Seated, he smiled at her. "You look well, Rebecca. I was not sure what to expect after two months in the village, but you look very well."

Becca sighed in satisfaction. Barnabas was a sight for sore eyes. She had wondered about him often, but there had been no word from anyone in Katmandu who knew him.

"How is your work?" Barnabas asked, glancing around the room. "Have the children accepted you?"

"The children are great. It's hard work to keep up with them; they're all different ages. Some of them don't care too much for school, so I have to make things interesting."

"Teaching is a gift. It is beautiful to see."

"I am the one who has received a gift," she said quietly.

"And life in the village? Are your accommodations satisfactory?"

She laughed. "Six months ago, I would have been horrified, but actually I have become quite accustomed to my little room. Even the lack of electricity does not bother me too much."

Barnabas smiled slyly. "How about the food?"

"It's hard to believe, but I've even gotten used to that. The missionary families eat the local dishes, so I do, too."

"We shall turn you into a true Nepali before you go home."

Becca smiled at the thought. "How long is your trip? Where are you staying?"

Barnabas patiently answered Becca's questions. He would have to move on to another village by nightfall. Their visit would be brief. Tomorrow he would reunite with his partner and continue working his way down the mountain, stopping in smaller places. Then he would return to Katmandu for another language and culture class. When that was finished, he hoped he would be back in Becca's area again, and he would try to stay longer.

While he spoke, Becca watched his face. The crinkles around

his blazing dark eyes and the animation of his mouth mesmerized her. She was strangely aware of her own heart beating—rapidly. Subtly she took a deep breath and tried to calm herself.

When the conversation lagged for a moment, Becca's thoughts went to the question that had been on her mind for weeks. "How is your family?" she asked tentatively.

"They are well," he answered. His eyes told her that he understood what she was asking. After a pause, he continued. "The wedding has been postponed."

Becca let out an involuntary sigh of relief; Barnabas continued. "The girl did not want to get married yet."

"Oh? But. . . ?"

"She is very young. Our parents agreed to wait one year before the wedding. They have not announced the engagement. Only the girl and her parents know of the arrangement."

Becca nodded slowly, not sure of what to say. She stared out the window.

"Well, this is good news," she said finally, "for now."

"For now. The extra time is a gift from the Lord. Many things can change in a year."

"I suppose so." She thought of how much her life had changed in just a few months. Would it change even more? "Have you spoken with her?" she asked softly, wondering what a young girl might be feeling at the prospect of being married off to someone she hardly knew.

Barnabas shook his head. "I have not been to Pokhara. I think it is better if I do not go there."

"But that means you can't see your family, either," Becca said.

"My uncle brings news when he comes to Katmandu. That is enough for me."

"This is a horrible situation!" she cried, unable to guard her frustration any longer.

"Rebecca, please do not be distressed. The Lord is present."

She turned her face back to him. "I don't know another person in the world who can be so calm in the face of the problem you have. Certainly not me."

"Normally, engagements and marriages happen very quickly in Nepal," Barnabas explained. "The Lord has already shown His power by delaying the wedding. He will make His way clear."

"But your parents. . . ?" She choked on the rest of her sentence.

"Yes, my parents. They believe they are thinking of my best interests. But they are not stronger than God."

Becca let her shoulders sag. "Okay, Barnabas. I will try not to worry so much."

Barnabas reached into his shirt pocket. "I have brought some letters for you."

"Mail?" Excitedly she hopped off the little desk and reached for the envelopes.

"They arrived at the mission house some time ago. When I learned that the plane was not coming to you this week, I brought them."

"Thank you. This makes your visit even brighter." There were three letters, one each from her parents, Karen, and Dan.

The porch door swung open again, and David Bridgman entered. "Barnabas! The children told me they saw you come up the hill."

Barnabas grinned and reached out to shake David's hand.

"You haven't been up this way in almost two years," David said. "What has brought you now?"

Glancing toward Becca, Barnabas answered. "We are starting a new work nearby. Some of the people in your agriculture project are ready to listen to our recordings, so I have come."

"Well, this is wonderful. I hope we will see you more often now."

"I hope to include this area on a regular route." Again he glanced at Becca. She met his eyes.

"Why don't you come and say hello to Sandy? She'll be delighted to see you."

Barnabas turned to Becca. "Will you excuse me?"

She smiled and waved the letters in her hand. "I'll read these, and then we can talk again in a little bit."

After David and Barnabas left, Becca ripped open the letter from her mother. She knew it would be full of news from home and not demand a taxing response. Scanning it, she smiled at the familiar references and the humorous innuendos that made up her mother's writing style.

She was not sure whether to read Karen's letter next, or Dan's. Karen was probably reacting to Becca's letter describing Barnabas. Dan's would be obliviously innocent. Deciding to get the challenging one over first, Becca broke the seal on Karen's letter.

Dear Becca,

Just got your first letter. It took most of a month to reach me. Phil almost did not want to give it to me because he knew I would stop cooking dinner to read it and he was hungry!

Nepal sounds like such a mixture of beauty and grim reality. We've lived such insulated lives, you and I, in the suburbs of middle America. Even the crime report from the inner city sounds like another culture, one that we don't expect to experience. How you are coping with everything that you have described is beyond me. Hopefully, your cultural orientation course helps.

Now, about this Barnabas fellow. When you said you wanted an adventure, I had no idea this is what you had in mind! My first reaction was to shout, "Are you out of your mind?" But I didn't. (Phil would have thought I was talking to him;

he's used to hearing me say that.) But then I read again what you had written about him, and I began to see things from a different perspective.

Becca, you know I think the world of Dan, and personally I think the two of you would live quite happily ever after. At least that's what I thought up until your letter. Now I realize that it is not up to me to sit around, dreaming about your life. I know Dan is anxious for you two to get married when you get back next year, and I was, too. But what matters is how you feel. And obviously you have doubts.

At the same time, though, I wonder how much your feelings are influenced by where you are right now—in Nepal. It sounds to me like Barnabas was your lifeline during your language and culture course. But how well do you really know him? If you weren't pulled away from everything familiar to you, would you still feel the same way about him?

I don't pretend to have answers. I'm just asking questions. And we know each other well enough that I ask them sincerely.

I have to tell you about the new editor at work.

From there on, Karen's letter drifted into the details of her office relationships, an ongoing soap-operalike saga that had amused Becca for a long time. No doubt later she would chuckle at the rest of the letter. For now, she folded it up and slipped it back into the envelope.

Karen had raised some legitimate questions. How well did Becca really know Barnabas? Only a few minutes ago they had danced verbally around the subject of his engagement, neither one of them expressing what was on both their minds. If they could not even talk freely about their feelings for each other, then perhaps their friendship was not so strong as she had thought.

Now she had to face the most awkward of the three letters. With her lips pressed together, she opened Dan's envelope.

Dear Becca,

Thanks for your letters—I've received two since I last wrote you. You've tried your best to describe where you are, but I have to admit that it's difficult for me to picture a village on the side of a mountain in Nepal. I saw Karen at church and she showed me the pictures you sent. That helped. But then it was even harder to imagine you, living there. I must have asked you a half a dozen times to try camping with our group and you never would. Now you live in a place without running water and with questionable electricity.

I ran into the principal from your school the other day. She remembered me from the Christmas dinner last year and asked how you were doing. She's pretty sure there will be an opening on the school staff next year, and she's anxious to have you come back. But you might have to teach fifth grade instead of third.

Of course, you won't have to work at all, if you don't want to. I just got a promotion and a big fat raise to go along with it.

Dan went on to tell her about his new responsibilities, but what riveted Becca was his underlying assumption that they would marry. Until recently she had shared that assumption, even if in a half-hearted way. They had talked about it on numerous occasions. How could she possibly write to him from halfway around the world and tell him she was having second thoughts? What if Karen was right? What if her curious affection for Barnabas was simply because she was in Nepal instead of home in Porter?

The porch door creaking open again startled her. "Everything okay?" Barnabas asked, as she looked up at him.

"Yes, fine."

"Good news from home?"

"Everything seems to be fine. I guess Porter can get along without me after all." As she slipped Dan's letter out of sight under Karen's, she changed the subject. "How much longer can you stay?"

"Only a few minutes, I'm afraid."

Trying not to sound disappointed, Becca said, "Were you serious about this area being on a regular route?"

Barnabas nodded. "I will come again next month. After that we will know more about how the work is going."

❧

That night Becca lay in bed, struggling to relax. Her mind told her that what she felt about Barnabas was ridiculous. She had a steady, time-tested relationship with Dan. She knew what the future held if she married him.

Barnabas, though, was unknown in many ways. Only once had he said anything to make her think that their relationship was more than friendship. But that one time, on the day his uncle had come to the school, was all it took to make her mind spin.

eleven

Barnabas did come again the next month, and the month after that. Each time he stayed overnight in the village and they spent the days together.

Sitting behind her big desk, Becca looked at her watch at two-minute intervals, aching for the time to pass until Barnabas arrived that afternoon. As the children worked quietly, Becca idled over some arithmetic worksheets that needed correcting. Concentrating on anything seemed impossible just then. When she had left Katmandu, she had not imagined she would see Barnabas until she returned to the city for a brief break midway through her term, probably at Christmastime. Now she counted the days until she thought he might come. Soon he would begin another tutoring session and would not be free to travel. This might be his last visit for a few weeks.

In the spirit of their friendship, they did as they had done in Katmandu and walked as they talked. The first time they had walked down the dirt main street together had drawn stares from the villagers. What did this striking young Nepali have in common with the American teacher? At first, Becca had been self-conscious about their strolls. In Katmandu, their relationship had been hidden behind their work together as tutor and student. In the village they had no such shield; friendship, not work, brought them together. Barnabas seemed not to mind the stares from the villagers or the smiles from the missionaries. Becca decided to follow his lead. Finding a private place to converse in the village was difficult, but if they hiked up the hillside, they could be alone and talk freely.

Another glance at her watch revealed that Becca could safely dismiss the class for the day. Their books slammed shut and papers fluttered around for a moment while everyone got organized. Then they were gone. Only one student, Jill Bridgman, remained.

"Do you need help with something?" Becca asked as Jill walked toward her with an open folder.

"I just have a question about this lesson for the Nepali girls. Can you look at it?"

"Sure, what's the problem?" Becca bent her head over the papers that Jill offered her, and together they sorted out the lesson plan Jill would use later that afternoon.

"You've really stuck with this, Jill," Becca said. "You should be proud of what you have accomplished."

Jill was proud; Becca could see it in her eyes. At the same time, a shadow crossed Jill's face. "I just wish more girls would come. Only seven come, and some of them not all the time."

Becca shook her head. "I know. In the States we take it for granted that girls will go to school. But around here. . ."

"They say their fathers don't see any reason girls should learn to read. And they have too much work to do. They go with their mothers to do laundry in the stream."

"Concentrate on the ones who do come," Becca advised, touching Jill's shoulder. "From what I can see, they are making good progress."

Jill brightened a bit. "Yes, they are. A couple of them can read whole stories already, as long as I keep the vocabulary simple."

For a moment, neither of them spoke. "Is there something else?" Becca asked, not wanting to be rude but watching the clock.

"I do have another question. But it's not about school or the reading group."

"What is it?"

"Is it really okay to ask?"

"Of course."

Jill hesitated and looked down at her feet. "My dad said Barnabas is coming again today. Are you waiting for Barnabas?"

Becca was startled by the question but answered promptly. "Yes, I am." She tried to get Jill to look her in the eye. "Why do you ask that, Jill?"

The girl clutched her folder to her chest. "Some of the villagers . . .well, they've been watching, and they think. . ."

"They think what?" Becca gently prompted.

"They think you have a strange friendship with Barnabas. He is a Nepali and you are an American who will go home next year."

"I can have friends while I'm here, can't I?" Becca said softly and evenly.

"Well, yes, but that's not what they think. They think you and Barnabas. . . Well, in the States, we would call it dating." Now Jill lifted her head and looked at Becca. "Is that what you are doing? Are you having dates with Barnabas?"

Becca forced herself to breathe slowly. She looked into Jill's questioning brown eyes and knew she could not skirmish around the truth. But what was the truth?

"Barnabas and I have a unique relationship," she began. "When I first came to Nepal, I needed his help with a lot of things. That meant that we spent a lot of time together."

"But he doesn't come here to help you. He comes here just to visit, doesn't he?"

"Yes, that's true. We enjoy each other's company, and we have become good friends along the way."

"My parents think Barnabas should get married," Jill said abruptly. "They really like him, and they think he would be happy if he got married."

Becca chose her words carefully. "That might be true. What Barnabas wants to do most of all is obey God. When God shows him that it is time to get married, I'm sure he will."

"You didn't really answer my question about dates," Jill said.

"You are asking some complicated questions," Becca replied.

"I'm sorry," the girl muttered. "I don't mean to be rude. I'm just wondering."

"I understand. And I'm glad you felt like you could ask me. But I'm afraid I don't have all the answers."

"I'd better go," Jill said. "The girls will be waiting."

Becca nodded. "Let me know how it goes."

Jill left, and Becca fell back into her chair. The girl had asked questions that echoed the ones flying around Becca's mind. She and Barnabas simply walked and talked. They did not go out to dinner or to concerts or any of the things that she did with Dan. But she had no doubt in her mind that every time they met they were building a relationship that was becoming more and more important to both of them.

❧

Becca and Barnabas hiked for more than three hours that afternoon, sometimes talking, sometimes being companions in silence. Twigs crunched under their feet, and rocks knocked loose by their steps, scuffled in the dirt. The scent of the forest filled Becca's nostrils deliciously, and she breathed its sweetness deeply.

"I love this mountain," she said after a period of comfortable silence. "I try to describe it for my friends at home, but I never find the right words."

"It is the handiwork of God," said Barnabas, "and that is beyond words."

"If only there were some way to stop the deforestation," Becca said sadly. The grandeur of the mountain was being stripped away day by day, tree by tree, as villagers up and down the mountain cut wood for cooking and warmth. Enormous patches of exposed earth blighted the dense greenery. Becca knew that the utilitarian value of the wood would always dominate the mountain as a natural wonder. The people of the mountain were too poor and overworked to worry about where the next generation would get its wood.

"It will be dark soon," Barnabas said. "Perhaps we should turn back."

"Let's stay just a few more minutes," Becca pleaded.

Barnabas gestured to a fallen log. "We can sit here and rest."

They sat side by side, gazing out at the valley before them. The late afternoon sun flooded the basin with golden light, casting a magical hue over the land.

"I received a letter from a school in the U.S.," Barnabas said softly, after a few minutes.

Becca's head snapped around excitedly. "Have you been accepted?"

"Provisionally. I am not yet sure when I will be able to go. There are many factors to consider."

Becca sighed. "Like your engagement?"

"Yes."

"Have you spoken to your parents about it recently?"

"Yes," he said again. "I have asked them to consider allowing me to marry someone other than the girl they have chosen."

Becca's eyes widened as she listened.

"My mother insists that I must do as they decide. But my father has finally agreed that I am free to marry whomever I choose. However, if I do not take the wife they have chosen, they will not provide the funds for my training."

"So nothing has changed."

"I am still trusting God."

"But Barnabas, if you marry that woman—"

Barnabas cut her off quietly. "I will not marry her."

"You mean. . . ?"

"I have chosen another."

Becca's stomach flip-flopped. She fumbled for words. "I. . .I didn't know. . . I'm pleased for you, of course. Is it someone in Katmandu?"

Barnabas smiled. "No, Rebecca. It is a gentle, kind woman who lives in a little village on the side of a mountain. I would like to marry you."

"Me? You want to marry me?"

"Perhaps I have overstepped my bounds." Barnabas looked down at his hands nervously. "But I would like for us to marry and serve the Lord together."

Becca's heart pounded as she tried to think of what to say. Despite her growing feelings toward Barnabas, she had not allowed herself to dream that this moment would come. She was not prepared.

"I am very fond of you, Barnabas," she said at last. "You have been one of the truest people I have ever known. Every moment that we are together makes me happy. But are you sure of what you are asking? Marrying an American. . .would your family ever speak to you again?"

"I know that such a marriage would not be without complications," Barnabas answered. "You, too, would be making a sacrifice. And I have no right to ask you to make such a sacrifice. But I am convinced that marrying you would be the right thing to do, so I am content to put the outcome into God's hands."

Becca stood up and began to pace nervously across the small clearing.

"Have I surprised you with this?" Barnabas asked. "Although we have not spoken directly about this subject, I hoped it had been in your thoughts as well."

"Yes, I have thought of it," Becca answered. "But it is such a complicated question. . .and I was not sure of your feelings."

"I was wrong not to speak honestly before this. I'm sorry if I have caused you to suffer—"

"Oh, no," Becca protested, "you have done nothing wrong."

Barnabas continued. "I only wished to be sure before I said anything to you. If I am to marry you, it must be because God has brought us together, not because I wish to escape a traditional marriage to a girl from my village."

"And are you sure?" She stopped pacing and looked at him.

Barnabas nodded solemnly. "But you must also be sure." He stood up, faced her, and took her hands in his. His dark eyes bore right through her, and she quivered. "You must have some time to pray. Please, do not be hurried by what I have said or by my family circumstances."

All Becca could manage was a nod. She needed time to think . . .and pray.

❧

That night, Becca did not sleep well. At dinner with the Bridgman family, she had managed to sit across from Barnabas and behave normally. Later, Barnabas had walked her back to her small house and said good night like a perfect gentleman, with no mention of their previous discussion. When the generator went off, she did not light a candle. She sat in the dark for a long, long time. She ached to be able to pick up a phone and call Karen to talk through her feelings. But there was no phone in the village. She was on her own this time.

If she married Barnabas, they would find a way for him to go to the States, even without his parents' blessing and support. Maybe it would even be easier for Barnabas to go if he were married to an American citizen. She could teach and provide their support while he studied. But he would not want to stay. His whole reason for going to the States was simply to be trained as a pilot so he could return to his own country to reach remote areas with the news of Jesus. He would never settle for a comfortable life in the U.S.

Was Becca prepared to spend her life in Nepal? To isolate herself indefinitely from her own family and friends? To raise a family under the difficult circumstances that characterized life even in Katmandu?

And what if Karen was right? What if her feelings for Barnabas were because she was in Nepal and not home in Porter? She had not even mentioned Dan to Barnabas, and perhaps that was unfair. Would he have nurtured their relationship as he had if he had known she was practically engaged herself? She had not been honest with him; keeping secrets was no foundation for marriage.

She tried to pray, to approach her relationship with Barnabas as a question of faith in God's leading as Barnabas had done. But her questions persisted, and she had no peace. She dozed off, exhausted, only to be tormented by dreams of gray hallways and spiderwebs and disemboweled dogs run over by taxis.

At last dawn crept across the sky and sneaked through the tiny windows in her bedroom. With relief, Becca got out of bed and rummaged for some fresh clothing. Breakfast was a long time off, and she could not stand being cooped up in her room. She would take a long hike, burn off some energy. Perhaps she could pray up on the mountain.

When she came back down, Barnabas had just emerged from breakfast. He smiled at her and welcomed her. "We missed you at breakfast."

"I went for a walk."

"It is a beautiful morning for a walk." He paused, then said, "I hope your walked accomplished what you hoped for."

"Barnabas," Becca said, determined to be forthright. "I didn't sleep at all last night. I couldn't stop thinking about our talk yesterday and all the questions it stirs up."

Barnabas raised his eyebrows and listened.

"I haven't been honest with you," Becca said softly.

His face fell. "You do not share my feelings?"

"Yes, I do. At least I think I do. But there is something I have not told you about."

"Ah, I see."

Becca swallowed and forced herself to continue. "There is a man back home. His name is Dan."

"And you are. . .committed to him?"

"He wants to marry me when I'm finished with my year here."

Barnabas nodded silently, understanding. He asked no questions but allowed Becca to say as much or as little as she wished.

"When I came to Nepal, I assumed I would go home and get married. But things are different now. Since I've met you, I'm not sure I can marry Dan. But I can't promise that I will marry you, either. . .at least not soon enough to persuade your parents to call off your engagement. There are so many things to think about."

"I see. Of course I would not want you to do something that you are not sure of."

"I'm sorry, Barnabas," she said, her voice almost a whisper. "You are so sure that God is leading us together. I feel terrible that I cannot be confident of the same thing. My faith is not as strong as yours."

"Please, do not feel badly, Rebecca. At least we have spoken honestly with each other. And if it truly is God's will, then He will assure your heart."

She looked at him, tears brimming in her eyes. "Do you have any idea how much I admire you? When you say those things, I can see that you really believe them."

"Of course I do." Their eyes locked together.

"I'll understand if you don't want to come visit anymore." She choked on a sob as she forced the words out.

Barnabas nodded silently. "Perhaps that would be best. . .for a while."

Becca could contain herself no longer. She turned and ran to her room to cry.

twelve

Becca's stomach grumbled as she sat in the grass surrounded by Nepali girls learning to read. Jill was teaching the lesson from a book she had made herself, complete with drawings and text. The story was about a little girl who did not like to obey her mother. Becca was impressed by Jill's ability to build a reading lesson around an everyday experience that the students could identify with. The girl was a gifted teacher, and since beginning the reading class project she had forgotten her doubts about whether she wanted to be in Nepal. Secretly, Becca envied Jill's resolute quality. Once she had a purpose of her own, Jill was content to be in Nepal instead of in an American junior high school. Becca's doubts, however, persisted.

Three weeks had passed since her last conversation with Barnabas. She doubted that he would be coming to the village again. Becca was determined to complete her commitment to teach for one year; beyond that, promises were hard to make. Though her heart felt like stone, she believed she had done the right think to tell Barnabas the truth and not throw herself into a situation she was unsure of. Shading her eyes, she glanced at her watch as her stomach rumbled once more. Thirty minutes until time for dinner.

She was surprised to see David Bridgman stride across the clearing. No one ever disturbed their work with the little girls, and his posture signaled that this was no casual visit. Intuitively she jumped up and left the circle to meet David.

"What is it, David? Is Sandy all right?"

"Yes, yes, everything's fine here. But I'm afraid I have some bad news for you."

"What do you mean?" Immediately Becca thought something had happened to Barnabas.

"The plane just came in, and the pilot brought a message from your mother. She called the mission house, and Harriett wrote it down."

Her heart thudded in her chest. "What's wrong?"

"Here, you can read it yourself." David thrust a crumpled note toward her.

Becca scanned the page.

Dad had a major heart attack. The doctors say he is gravely ill and his only hope is surgery. But he is too sick for surgery. We will have to wait a few days and see if he is strong enough. Sorry to distress you at such a distance, but of course you had to know.

Love,
Mom

Looking at the date, she blurted, "This was three days ago!"

"I'm sorry it took so long to get the message to you. The plane had engine trouble and didn't make the usual run earlier in the week."

"David, I have to go home." Becca's words were an indisputable statement.

"Yes, of course you do," David agreed.

"I'm sorry about the children. I have lesson plans. . .maybe someone else. . . ."

David reached out and put a hand on her shoulder. "Please, don't waste energy worry about those things. We'll be fine. Concentrate on your own family right now."

Becca nodded mutely. The lump in her throat kept her from speaking further.

"The plane will be coming back through tomorrow morning

on its way back to Katmandu. I've already checked to see if there is a seat, and they are willing to give you priority status."

Becca nodded again.

"You'll have to be ready at six o'clock to walk down to the airstrip. Okay? I'll go with you, of course." David glanced over at the circle of girls. "Why don't you let Jill finish up here. I'll walk you back to the house. We can find some of the believers and pray for your father."

"I'd like that," Becca managed to say. She glanced at her watch again. In twelve hours she would be on her way to the States.

❧

Despite her earlier hunger, Becca picked at her dinner and did not really eat. Following the meal, missionaries and Nepali Christians gathered at the Bridgman house and prayed for an American man they did not know. Becca was comforted and better able to concentrate. After the prayer gathering, she got a grip on what she had to do. She had no idea how long she would be home, whether a few weeks or permanently. She laid open a suitcase on her bed and started sorting through the few belongings she had brought with her to Nepal. Pressing a hand to her forehead, she tried to think what the season would be like at home. It was November; it would be cold. Most of her warm clothes were stored at her parents' house; whatever she needed she could get there. In the end, she put the suitcase away and stuffed two changes of clothing and a sweater into her shoulder bag. That would have to do for now.

❧

Harriett Metcalf greeted her at the airport in Katmandu. Relieved to see a familiar face, Becca nearly fell into the older woman's arms. "I took the liberty of checking on flights," Harriett said. "I was sure you would want to go home for a few weeks."

Becca nodded. "As much as I hate to leave the children right now, I have to go. I'll come back as soon as I can."

"Take all the time you need," Harriett said. "Your family needs you."

Becca shifted her bag on her shoulder. "About the flights?"

"Oh, yes. You have a seat on a flight leaving tonight. I'm afraid it's full fare; there were no discounted seats left."

Becca waved away the concern. "That doesn't matter. Can I pay with a credit card?"

"Let's just step over to the ticket counter and see. Then you can come back to the mission house and rest for a few hours. Have you eaten anything today? We should be there in time for lunch."

Becca followed Harriett to the ticket counter, arranged her passage, and then collapsed into the torn-up back seat of a taxi.

After lunch, Harriett let her into an empty room and she tumbled onto the bed. Though exhausted, she was unable to sleep. Back in this familiar setting, she kept expecting Barnabas to appear in the dining room, and she found herself cocking her ear toward every sound that wafted up to her room. But he did not appear. She wrestled with calling the office of his organization to leave a message but forced herself to refrain. She had cut her ties with Barnabas; it would be unfair to lean on him right now. Still, she could not help wishing he would come through the door with his stalwart faith. She needed someone to show her how to believe.

When dinner time came, and it was morning in the States, she shut herself up in Harriett's office and dialed her home phone number.

"Hello?"

"Mom?"

"Becca! Did they reach you with my message?"

"Last night. I'll be on my way home in just a couple of hours."

"Oh, I'm so relieved."

"How's Dad?"

"Not any better. They think he needs a heart transplant."

"A transplant?"

"The damage from the heart attack was severe. The cardiologist suspects that his heart has not been working well for a long time."

Becca groaned and thought of all the times she and her mother had pleaded with her father to have regular medical checkups. "Is he on a list for a new heart?"

"Not yet. They have a few more tests to do to make sure he is a good candidate."

"But you just said—"

"He has to be well enough to survive another surgery, Becca." Her mother's voice was strained with reality.

Becca felt the color drain from her face. Her father was much more ill than she had imagined.

"I'll be home in about twenty-four hours," Becca said, helpless to know what else to say. She relayed her flight information to her mother, who promised to meet the plane. Sinking into the desk chair, she choked back her tears. It was time to go to the airport, not to coddle her emotions.

Becca insisted that Harriett did not need to come with her and took a taxi to the airport on her own. Standing in the customs line, she remembered the anxiety of her arrival day, the panic as she wondered if she had bitten off more than she could chew. Becca had part of her answer: she could handle the one-year commitment she had made and was grieved at the thought that she might not be able to return and fulfill it. But her months in Nepal had enlarged the question. Barnabas had spoken the challenge, and she had been unable to rise to it.

At last she was through the line, her passport stamped with a black exit stamp. She looked at the visa stamp she had received six months earlier and reminded herself that it was still good; she could come back. She displayed her ticket and exit stamp to the attendant and passed through the glass doors that separated passengers from well-wishers.

"Rebecca!"

Her head snapped around at the sound of his voice. As the doors slid closed, she saw Barnabas on the other side. She turned around and pressed against the flow of foot traffic. He thrust his shoulders through the crowd and kept his eyes on her.

An airport attendant shook his head; she would not be allowed to return to the waiting area. With her heart in her throat, she watched as Barnabas pleaded from the other side. But it was to no avail. Questions rankled in her mind: How did he know she was at the airport? How much information did he have? What did he want to say to her?

Resigned to the reality that they could not speak, she pressed one hand flat against the glass. Barnabas raised his and did the same, his fingers spread to meet the pattern of hers. His dark eyes held her searching gaze, but she found no answers. Simultaneously, their heads turned toward the loudspeaker as her flight was called. Barnabas stepped back from the glass, signaling that she should go. She looked at the hand, imagining that she could feel his touch. Then she turned around to find her way and, when she glanced over her shoulder once more, he was gone. The line of passengers closed in around her.

❧

The flight seemed interminable, even longer than her flight into Nepal. She did not sleep. She ate very little. She could not concentrate enough to read a magazine. During the course of the flight, three movies dominated the cabin. Her eyes faced the screen and she wore the headphones, but she would have been hard pressed to relay the plot of any of the films. Never before had she felt in such a stupor.

What if her father were not well enough for transplant surgery? What if a heart did not become available soon enough? What if he did not get well? Would she ever return to Nepal? Were her experiences there to be swallowed up in the realities of life in the States as if they had never happened? If she came back to Nepal, could she treat Barnabas as if their relationship had never happened?

The plane's landing was one of the smoothest she had ever experienced. She was safe and sound on U.S. soil again. She had passed through customs in Los Angeles and changed planes for the flight to Cleveland. There, the skyline looked familiar and strange at the same time. When the seat belt sign went off, Becca retrieved her bag and joined the crowd in the aisle. She scanned the arrival area, looking for her mother. Instead, she saw Dan.

He moved toward her, sporting a moustache he had not had six months ago. "Hello, Becca." Before she knew it, he had wrapped his arms around her and begun kissing her.

"Dan!" she said when he finally released her. "What a surprise. My mom said she would meet my plane."

"I talked her out of it," he said. "I didn't think she should be driving this far in her emotional state, and I don't think she wanted to leave your dad."

"When did you talk to her?" Becca was still trying to put the pieces together.

"This morning. Karen told me about your dad right away, so I've been in touch with your family. Your brother's here, too."

"Andy?" Andy had not been home from Texas for almost three years. "Too bad it takes an emergency to get him to come home for a visit."

"Don't get on his case now, Becca," Dan warned. "I know the two of you haven't gotten along lately, but the last thing your mother needs is to play referee between you and Andy."

"You're right, of course."

Dan took her bag off her shoulder and they started walking toward the parking lot.

"How is my father? Any better."

Dan shook his head. "I'm afraid he's a bit worse. The doctor suspects he has pneumonia now."

Becca groaned. "Have you seen him?"

"No. He's in intensive care. Only family is allowed in."

"Is my mom there now?"

Dan nodded. "You did the right thing to come home, Becca. Your mom needs you. Andy is here, but. . ."

"Andy is Andy," Becca said bluntly.

"Give him a break."

When they reached the car, Dan unlocked the passenger door and held it open for her. Automatically she inspected the seat for rips or loose springs; there were none. She chuckled under her breath at how ingrained a six-month-old habit had become.

Dan got settled in and they were underway. Snow covered the ground, but the sun had melted random patches and cars had soiled the edges of the snowbanks. Becca thought of the pristine vision of the Himalayan snowcaps, where no exhaust fumes ever went. She shivered in her sweater. As if reading her mind, Dan reached into the back seat and handed her a blanket. "Sorry," he said, "I didn't think about your coat."

"That's okay," she said, gratefully spreading the blanket across her body. "Neither did I."

Traffic was orderly, everyone stayed in the designated lanes, and even after thirty minutes she had not heard a single horn blare. The only cows were in the pastures on the farms outside Porter. Everything was familiar, yet somehow Becca felt out of place.

thirteen

Becca gently pushed the door open and peered into the intensive care area. Ashen and still, her father was almost unrecognizable. Her mother sat in a chair at the side of the bed, her head slumped down on her chest and a book upside down in her lap.

"Mom," Becca said softly. There was no response. Becca stared at her mother and soaked up every familiar feature. Somehow her mother seemed more gray and thin than Becca remembered. She told herself it was because of the stress of her father's illness, but she could not help wondering if her mother was well. She walked quietly around the bed and knelt in front of her mother.

"Mom," she repeated, taking her mother's hand.

Sarah Masterson's eyes fluttered open weakly, and she seemed not to focus for a moment. At last she said, "Becca. You're home."

"Yes, Mom, I'm here. I'm home."

As they embraced, Becca once again thought that her mother seemed thin. "Are you all right, Mom?" she asked. "You must be exhausted."

Her mother only nodded.

"Have you slept in a bed at all since this started."

Sarah shook her head. "I only leave him when I have to. I was so glad when Dan offered to meet your flight."

"Mom, are you hungry? When was the last time you ate?"

A twinkle glazed Sarah's eyes. "I should be asking you these questions, Becca."

Becca smiled and tried to smooth her unruly hair. "You're right. What a mess we both are." She turned to look at her father. "How's Dad? Anything new?"

"He's still very ill. But they think he's a bit better. The pneumonia seems to be under control."

"Is he stable enough for surgery?"

Sarah shook her head. "They don't know yet."

"What about a donor heart?"

"He's on the national list with a priority status."

"What does that mean?"

Sarah's eyes drifted from her daughter to her husband. "We hope that it means he won't have to wait as long as a lot of other people have."

Becca turned around to pick up her father's hand and squeeze it. "If only it were a kidney or bone marrow or something we could give him. I would do it in a minute."

"I know you would, sweetie. So would I. But we can't, so we just have to trust God's timing."

"Does Dad know you're here? Does he wake up?"

"Only for a few minutes at a time. That's why I hate to leave. I want him to see me here whenever he is awake. I don't want him to be alone."

"I can sit with him, Mom, so that you can get some decent rest."

"I can't sleep."

"You can at least lie down for a while or maybe grab a shower."

Sarah nodded reluctantly. "Perhaps later."

"Dan said Andy was home," Becca said. "Where is he now?"

"I'm not sure. At the house, I suppose."

Becca stifled the rage welling up inside her. "Has he been here at all?"

"He stopped in the first day he got here. But since Dad is asleep so much of the time. . ."

"He's probably using this trip home as an excuse to see his buddies."

"Please, Becca. Everyone has to deal with this differently. I don't expect Andy, or you, to sit here constantly just because I choose to."

"This is not like deciding what you want on a pizza! Why can't

Andy think about someone besides himself?"

"Becca, you're not being fair. You haven't even seen him yet."

A nurse approached and took her father's pulse. Becca was awkwardly aware that she had allowed her voice to grow louder.

"This is my daughter," Sarah said to the nurse.

The nurse nodded. "Of course she is free to visit whenever she wants to, but please try to remain quiet."

"I'm sorry," Becca muttered. With a lowered voice, she turned back to her mother. "I'll make you a deal, Mom. Let's find the cafeteria and get something to eat—both of us. I promise I won't say anything else about Andy. Then we'll work out a plan so that one of us is here all the time."

"What about Dan? Is he waiting for you?"

Becca had forgotten about him, sitting in the waiting room because only family members were allowed into intensive care.

"He can come and eat with us," Becca said, "and then take one of us home."

"You go on with him," Sarah said. "You've come halfway around the world."

"We'll figure that out later. Let's just get something to eat."

❧

Two hours later, Becca reluctantly left her mother at her father's bedside once again. Becca had never seen her mother so stubborn. Fear for her husband's condition fueled her willfulness, and she would not bend to Becca's suggestion that she should go home while Becca kept watch. But she did agree to sleep in her own bed that night in exchange for her daughter's promise to stay at the hospital. So in the end it was Becca who rode home in Dan's car.

"You're pretty quiet," Dan said as he pulled out of the parking lot.

Becca shrugged. "It's a lot to absorb."

"Please understand my intentions," Dan said, "but I think your mother looks terrible."

Becca nodded agreement. "Getting her to the cafeteria was a small miracle, but she barely touched her food."

"She needs you."

"She needs more than I can give," Becca murmured. "She's terrified. I am, too."

"Of course you are," Dan said. "You're both under tremendous pressure. But things will work out."

Becca considered Dan's profile as he kept his eyes on the road in front of him. She liked the moustache, she decided. She was thankful for his help today, and he cared for her family in a genuine way. He was probably right; one way or another, things would work out. But the phrase struck her as feeble. Barnabas, she knew, would have said that God would work His way even in circumstances that seemed hopeless.

Dan pulled the car into the Masterson driveway and turned off the ignition.

"You don't need to go in with me," Becca said.

"Are you sure?"

"I'm just going to crash."

Dan looked at his watch. "I probably should get back to the office. I'll call you later, okay?"

Becca nodded.

"Maybe in a couple of days we'll have a chance to really talk. We have a lot to catch up on."

Again, Becca nodded. What would she say to Dan when the time came? She was too confused to know her own feelings.

Dan leaned over and kissed her cheek. "Bye." She got out and waved as he backed out onto the street.

Close to collapsing from her own exhaustion, she wanted only to take a hot shower and try to sleep before relieving her mother at the appointed time. With her shoulder bag in tow, she let herself in the back door and stepped into the kitchen.

She had lived all her life in that house, up until she went away to college. Even then she always found comfort from its familiar confines. It was not a large house. When she was in high school her parents had toyed with the idea of buying a larger one, but somehow they never made a final decision. After Becca and her brother were both on their own, there seemed to be no reason to move. Her mother had taken a modest and nondescript tract house and transformed it into a secure haven that neither of her parents wanted to leave. Becca understood their feelings. While she enjoyed having her own apartment before going to Nepal, she never hesitated to drop in at her parents' house when she longed for something familiar and stable.

Through her bleary eyes, she now inspected the kitchen. The white walls, carefully trimmed with a stenciled blue border, were cleaner and brighter than anything she had seen in months. She flipped the light switch just to reassure herself that the electricity was working. A drop from the gleaming faucet promised her that there would be running water. An image of the inviting double bed in her old room upstairs massaged her mind.

The drip pulled her her attention to the sink, which was occupied by a pile of unwashed dishes. Empty pop cans and potato chip bags cluttered the counters. Something in the trash had a most unpleasant odor. She sighed and let her shoulders sag. Andy was definitely home.

Hoisting her bag on her shoulder, she headed through the dining room toward the stairs. Andy sat in the living room, transfixed in front of the television.

"Hello, Andy," Becca forced herself to say.

He turned his head but did not get up. "I heard you were coming home. Did you get that missionary stuff out of your system?"

"I'm glad that you were able to get here, too," Becca said evenly. "I'm really bushed right now. I didn't sleep on the plane at all. I'll catch up with you later."

"Is Mom coming home?" Andy crushed an empty pop can in his fist.

"I'm going back to the hospital later to sit with Dad so she can come home and rest."

"How is the old guy?"

"Why don't you go down there and see for yourself?"

"What's that supposed to mean?" Andy finally got up and turned to face her.

Becca wished she had held her tongue. "Nothing."

"Don't give me that. You can't pass up an opportunity to stick a knife in me."

"Andy, give me a break. I just flew halfway around the world. I need to get some rest."

"Don't give me that!" he repeated.

"Look, Andy, I know you must be worried about Dad or you would not have come home from Texas. Let's just leave it at that, okay?" She started for the stairs once again.

"Well, thank you for that tiny concession."

"I'm not interested in fighting. Do you want to come back to the hospital with me later?"

"I'll think about it." He sank into his recliner again.

"It would mean a lot to Mom. . .and Dad, too, if he wakes up."

"Don't start on me, Becca."

Without replying, Becca began climbing the steps. At the top, she turned to the left and stepped into her old room and sank onto the bed. She had not been home for five minutes and had already encountered conflict with her only sibling. If he continued to express his feelings for their father, whatever they were, by watching television and cluttering the kitchen, Becca would undoubtedly spend most of her time away from the house.

Why couldn't they get along, especially at a time like this? Six years older than Becca, Andy had always been a mystery. The two of them had never really connected, except to squabble, even when they were children. Then Andy reached an age where he paid no attention to Becca, and she had come to prefer that.

What she did not like, though, was the turmoil her parents experienced because of Andy. She could remember the screaming rage of Andy's adolescence. Later, he learned to control his temper and moderate his public behavior, but inwardly he seethed with rebellion. When he moved away to Texas, the family had breathed a collective sigh of relief that the torment of regular encounters would be restrained by distance.

In the six years since he had moved away, none of Andy's rare visits home had been what Becca would consider successful. She had either avoided him completely to stay clear of the scuffle, or she would plop herself between Andy and her father as a buffer zone. Neither effort had proved profitable in restoring family relationships. Her mother had looked on forlornly, futilely wishing that her husband and her son could find peace with each other.

Suddenly, Becca gave way to an internal tidal wave and began to sob. Her father's illness frightened her beyond words; her mother's need for support overwhelmed her; her brother's presence enraged her, despite her best efforts; and it was only a matter of time before she would have to square off with Dan.

She reached toward the spot where she knew from habit that there would be a box of tissues and she wiped her nose. Taking a deep breath, she told herself that she could not afford to give in to any of those feelings. She looked around the room and remembered the way she used to come up here and play her stereo for hours, blocking out everything around her. She would tell her mother she was not hungry for dinner and then dive into her stash of snacks so she would not have to encounter the world outside her room. But she could not block out what was happening now, none of it.

To her own surprise, she heard herself say, "I miss you, Barnabas. You would know what to say right now."

Barnabas faced grave problems of his own. But somehow he was not rattled the way she was. "God will work it out," she had heard him say countless times, and she knew he believed it. But did she?

fourteen

"Becca, is that you?" her father asked.

"Yes, Dad, I'm here."

Rousing herself at the sound of his voice, Becca grasped her father's hand and gently positioned herself at the side of his bed. Wrinkles sagged around his jaws and neck in a way she had never noticed before. She did not think of him as an old man, but now he looked old.

"Have you been here all night?" he asked.

"Yes, but it's almost morning." She glanced toward the window.

"You should go home and get some sleep."

"I will. . .when Mom gets here."

"The two of you are going to collapse from exhaustion."

"Dad, we just want to be with you."

"You should take care of yourselves." His eyes closed and he drifted off to sleep again.

Becca sat quietly, still holding his hand and studying his features. His pale, thin face showed the effect of his body's battle for life and health. In the last few days, since Becca got home, her father had stabilized and was awake for long portions of the day. The pneumonia was under control and the doctors were optimistic that he would soon be fit enough for surgery—if a heart became available.

Despite sitting up in a chair most of the night, Becca was not all that tired. She had been home only four days; her body was still functioning on Nepal time, where it was now early evening.

For four days Becca had traded bedside shifts with her mother. Andy had dropped by occasionally but never stayed more than a few minutes, convinced that his presence meant little. He had told Becca he was thinking about going back to Texas before he used up all of his vacation time on one trip. Andy had made the most of being home to see old friends and indulge in whatever satisfied him at the moment. Becca did not know what to think of his perfunctory visits to the hospital; maybe it would be just as well if he went back to Texas.

The door creaked open and her mother entered. Becca got up and welcomed her with a kiss on the cheek. "How's he doing?" her mother asked.

"He had a good night. Slept for a long time. He was awake just a few minutes ago."

"I'm sure he was glad to see you. He was wishing you could come home for the holidays."

Becca shook her head. "But this is not what he had in mind."

"They'll be bringing his breakfast soon, I suppose."

Becca started. "Breakfast! I almost forgot. I told Dan I would meet him for pancakes before he goes to work."

"You'd better get going so you can freshen up."

Becca ran a hand through her scraggly hair and looked at the clock. "Maybe I have time to run home for a quick shower."

❧

Becca looked with relief at the strong, black coffee the waitress set in front of her. Dan laughed.

"Looks like you really need that," he said.

She lifted the warm mug and breathed in its aroma before sipping. "More than I like to admit."

"Did you sleep at all in your dad's room?"

She shook her head. "On and off. Not enough to count. It's amazing how busy a hospital is in the middle of the night."

"How's your jetlag?"

"About the same. I suppose staying up all night every night is not really helping my adjustment. But if I don't go over there at night, my mother will insist on staying. I don't want her to do that. It worries me."

"Do I dare ask about Andy?" Dan ventured. "Can't he help out?"

Becca rolled her eyes. "I brought it up once and was sorry I said anything. I don't know why he bothered to come home."

"He might be more worried about your dad than you think. Everybody expresses things differently."

Becca looked at Dan and smiled mildly. "Is that a gentle way of chastising my attitude?"

Dan shrugged. "I don't really know Andy very well. I only know what I've heard about him from you during the last two years."

"And I've probably biased you."

"Maybe I should come by the house and chat with him in person."

Becca shook her head. "No point in that. He's got a chip on his shoulder the size of New Jersey. He'd eat you alive."

"Come on. He can't be that bad."

"Well," Becca said, backing off, "maybe not quite. Everybody is so stressed out, it's hard to know what to think. I know Mom is glad he came home, but they barely speak to each other, so I don't really understand why."

The waitress returned with a pitcher of orange juice and two platters of buttermilk pancakes. As they doctored up their breakfast with liberal portions of genuine butter and blackberry syrup, Dan changed the subject.

"How often did you get a breakfast like this in Nepal?" he said.

"Not often enough," Becca responded, visualizing the dry toast and overly sweet tea that was the morning fare in the village. Without hesitation, she jabbed her fork into the stack for a first taste.

"You look like you lost weight over there."

"A little perhaps. Curried rice is not too fattening—not like this." She took another mouthful.

"It's good to see you enjoying something as simple as a plate of pancakes."

"Mmm." Becca's mouth was too full to respond.

"You could have pancakes every day, you know."

Becca swallowed. "I would balloon up in no time."

"Well, okay, you could have pancakes in moderation if you stayed here."

"Stayed here?"

"Sure. Stay here. It could be a long time before you dad is well again. You said yourself that Andy is no help. You have a lot of good reasons to stay here."

Becca stopped chewing. She could hardly believe what she was hearing. "I made a commitment, maybe not for the best reasons, but it is a promise. I have only six months left."

"Exactly. It's not like you were planning to live over there long term. What's happening to your students? You don't really know when you'll be able to go back. Maybe it would be better if the mission found someone to take your place."

Becca had to admit that she had not thought of the situation from the perspective of the mission. They had not questioned her need for an emergency leave, but they were left in the lurch. "It could take weeks to find someone. By the time they do, I'll be ready to go back anyway," she argued.

"You don't know that for sure. They found you pretty fast."

"But the regular teacher will be back from furlough in six months. It's not worth getting somebody involved for that short period of time."

Dan backed off. "I didn't mean to upset you."

"I know." She stabbed another bite of pancake and avoided looking at him.

"I was just looking at things realistically. Your family needs you."

She sighed heavily. "I know that, Dan. That's why I came

home. But as soon as Dad is well enough, I have to go back to Nepal."

"There are a lot of good reasons why you shouldn't. And I don't just mean your father's health."

Becca knew she had to choose her words carefully. "I have to finish what I started."

"What exactly did you start?" Dan asked softly.

Becca's stomach leaped to her throat. What did Dan know? Surely Karen had not told him about Barnabas.

"Well, for one thing, there's a girl named Jill who is having a tough time. I think I'm really helping her. She trusts me in a way she doesn't trust other adults." Becca paused to drink some coffee. "And there are all the other children. Their parents are filling in while I'm gone, but they have other things to do. They didn't become missionaries so they could home school their children in a strange country. I have a job to do."

"So you'll come home again when the year is up?" Dan searched her eyes with his.

"Of course," she said evenly, with only the slightest hesitation. "As soon as the regular teacher is back."

Dan nodded but did not speak.

I have to go back, Becca thought as she groped for words. What could she say to make Dan understand? Six months ago she had left in search of adventure and perhaps escape. Now it was something different pulling her back to the mountain kingdom of Nepal. But she had a hard time understanding it herself. How could she possibly explain it to him?

The waitress returned to refill their coffee mugs. Dan asked for more toast. From there, the meal quieted down, at least externally.

❧

Becca slept most of the day. Around noon, she heard Andy rummaging around the kitchen, just below her bedroom, but she did not rouse. At midafternoon, she got up, showered, and dressed. Thinking of the long night ahead of her, she stuffed a couple of paperbacks into an old backpack and turned her thoughts back to sitting up with her father. At five o'clock, the doorbell rang. She waited for Andy to answer it, but heard no movement. The bell sounded again and Becca headed down the stairs.

"Karen!" she said, opening the door. Knowing that her mind was still jetlagged some of the time, Becca panicked. "Was I supposed to meet you somewhere?"

"Oh, no, nothing like that," Karen assured her. "I just thought you'd like some dinner." She gestured at the grocery sack in her arms. "I have lasagna and garlic bread and a spinach salad."

"That does sound good," Becca admitted. "I haven't eaten since breakfast."

"Will your mom be home soon?"

Becca glanced at the clock. "I think so. She doesn't like to leave Dad, but if she doesn't come home for dinner, then we never see each other."

"Good. I brought enough for an army. Even including Andy."

Becca shrugged. "I don't know where he is."

"At the hospital, maybe," offered Karen.

"Not likely." Becca relieved Karen of the sack and headed toward the kitchen.

"Why didn't you eat lunch?"

"I was sleeping. Besides, I had a big breakfast this morning."

"With Dan? He told Phil he was meeting you."

"Maybe I'll put this in the oven to keep it warm until Mom comes home," Becca said, avoiding Karen's question.

"Aren't you and Dan getting along?" Karen persisted. Becca should have known better than to think Karen would be side-tracked so easily.

She shrugged. "It's a stressful time. He works during the day and I'm at the hospital at night. We haven't really seen much of each other."

Karen was not deterred. "With your dad in the hospital, this is no time to be figuring out your future, but I can't help thinking that you're not telling me everything."

Becca smiled and sighed at the same time. Karen's intuition was both charming and irritating.

"Have you heard from Barnabas?" Karen asked pointedly.

"Don't be ridiculous." Becca was quick to answer. She put the salad in the refrigerator.

"It's not ridiculous, if I'm to believe any of the letters you sent me." Karen perched on a kitchen stool; she was not moving until she had a satisfactory answer.

"Of course you can believe my letters."

"Then why don't I think I know the whole story?"

Becca busied herself starting the coffeepot. Then she turned to face Karen. "He came to the airport," she said quietly. "I hadn't seen him or talked to him since. . .since I told him I thought we shouldn't see each other again."

"How did he know you were at the airport?"

"I don't know. I had already passed through the customs area. We couldn't talk. We just looked at each other through the glass." But they had done more than look at each other. She thought of the way he had placed his palm against hers, with the glass between them. Their hearts had met when their words could not.

"What do you think that means?" Karen interrupted Becca's memory.

"What?"

"What do you think that means. . .that he came to the airport at the last minute?"

Becca shrugged. "I don't know. Friendship, I guess. Despite the way things turned out between us, I'd like to think we could be friends."

"I don't buy that," Karen said. "And I don't think you do, either."

Becca glanced at the clock and wished her mother would appear and rescue her from this tortuous conversation. She changed the subject. "Dan doesn't think I should go back," Becca said as she removed two coffee mugs from the cabinet.

"He never thought you should go in the first place."

"I know. And he seems determined to make sure I don't go back."

"Of course you have to go back." Karen's statement was simple and sincere. Becca was grateful for the support.

"Yes, I do have to go back. More than that, I want to go back. I haven't finished what I went over there to do."

"And Nepal hasn't finished with you, either."

"What do you mean?"

"I could tell from your letters that this experience is changing you," Karen said. "And now that I see you in person, I realize how different you are."

"Am I?"

Karen nodded. "If Dan can't see that. . ."

"I'm sure he wants to get married. . .soon."

"He's wanted that since the day you left. I'm surprised he hasn't booked the church and a reception hall already."

"I didn't tell Barnabas about Dan until the very end," Becca admitted. A tear escaped. "I always felt I was betraying Dan, but I couldn't help how I felt about Barnabas. It was as if Dan was not real, as long as Barnabas didn't know about him."

"What did he say when you told him?"

"I didn't give him a chance to say anything. I just said that I'd understand if he didn't want to see me anymore."

"You needed to see Dan again, Becca," Karen said. "You have to see the real Dan, and he has to see the real Becca. And then you have to see Barnabas again."

Becca nodded. "I know that now."

fifteen

Becca's father was asleep when she got to the hospital. She settled into a chair across the room and turned on a dim light so she could read. Out of her backpack she pulled a dog-eared mystery novel that she had read twice before. She hoped that its familiarity would lull her into dozing; instead, she found the story captivating because she noticed details she had not seen in previous readings.

Before she knew it, midnight had come. Setting the book aside, Becca stretched her arms over her head and yawned. Her father had been sleeping soundly for several hours. A nurse had come and checked the IV and his pulse, but the night had otherwise been uneventful. She glanced at her watch. Midnight in Ohio meant it was noon in Nepal. Repeatedly, she had found herself calculating the time difference and picturing the activities of her Nepal routine. It was just about time to dismiss the class for the midday consumption of curry and rice, perhaps with a few boiled potatoes. Was anyone even teaching the children? Was Jill keeping up with her lesson plans to teach Nepali girls how to read? Had Barnabas been to the village? By now he would have started tutoring in a new orientation program. She tried to picture him, his dark head bent over a grammar textbook, with a faceless student. What was he thinking about? Did he think about Becca?

Becca was considering to take a short walk down the hall, when the door opened. A shaft of light from the hall preceded a shadow of tentative footsteps. Andy stepped into the room. Becca looked at him, surprised.

"Hi," he said quietly.

"Hi." As far as Becca knew, her brother had never come to the hospital at night. What had brought him now?

"How is he?" Andy asked.

"He seems comfortable. He's been asleep since I got here." She paused. "Did you get anything to eat? Karen brought over some lasagne."

"Yeah. Mom heated some up for me."

"Are you on your way somewhere?" Even though it was midnight, Becca knew that Andy might very well be going to a party that was just starting.

"No," he said, surprising her again. "I just came to see how Dad is."

"He's better every day."

"That's good."

Becca gestured toward an empty chair. "Do you want to stay for a while?"

"Are you sure he won't wake up?"

"He usually sleeps through the night, until about five o'clock."

Andy lowered himself into the orange vinyl chair. "If he's asleep, then I guess it's safe to be here."

"What do you mean?" Becca asked.

"If he sees me, it will just upset him. And that won't be good for his heart."

"Is that why you stay away?" Becca asked, completely mystified by her brother's behavior at this point. "Because you think you upset him?"

"I don't think it, I know it." Andy kept his voice low, but his tone was adamant.

"It means a lot to both Mom and Dad that you came home from Texas because of Dad's illness."

"Maybe."

Becca persisted. "Not maybe. I know it's true."

"Becca, where have you been all of your life?" Andy was rolling his eyes dramatically. "You're six years younger than I am, but you're not an idiot."

"I don't know what you mean."

"You know Dad and I don't get along."

"Well. . . ," she struggled for words, unable to deny the truth of his statement. "You and Dad have your problems, I know, but I'm sure—"

"That underneath it all, he loves me. Is that what you were going to say?"

Becca did not answer; the words would have sounded artificial.

"I don't know if it's because you were a girl, or because you were younger, but you had it easy." Andy leaned forward with his elbows on his knees, looking at their father. "He didn't expect as much out of you. I was the son. I was supposed to do it all."

Becca hardly knew what to say. She had never heard Andy talk about this before and she was not sure why he decided to talk now, in the middle of the night in a hospital room while their father slept.

"You don't know what I'm talking about, do you?" Andy said, seeing her blank stare. He shook his head and sighed. "I don't suppose you would know. You were the daughter. You didn't have to do anything."

Resentment flared amid Becca's confusion. "Wait a minute. I worked hard through school and got my teaching certificate. I had a good job and an independent life when I decided to go to Nepal."

"And you think I don't? I was in the top ten percent of my college class, but I wasn't valedictorian. Dad never forgave me for that."

"That can't be true."

"It is. I messed around during high school. I don't deny that. Dad probably never even told you about the time that he had to bail me out of jail on a vandalism charge."

Becca shook her head. She knew nothing of the incident.

"You were only in fourth grade. He had to come and get me in the middle of the night. He wouldn't have told you."

"What happened?"

Andy shrugged. "It doesn't matter. It was a stupid, adolescent prank. But after that, Dad never looked at me the same way. He was ashamed of me from that day on. I straightened out, got good grades in college, landed a solid job when I graduated, but none of that mattered."

"Andy. . .I never knew."

"No, of course not. I'm just the brother who went astray. I couldn't redeem myself, no matter what I did. So when the chance came to transfer to Texas, I took it."

Becca realized at that moment that her parents had never gone to visit Andy in Texas, not once during the six years. She was beginning to understand why. "Are you happy in Texas?"

"Being happy doesn't have much to do with it. I had to get out from under the weight of Dad's disapproval."

"And did you?" Becca had decided that as long as Andy was answering questions, she would continue to ask them.

Andy shook his head. "Not really. I just feel like I've been exiled. At least Dad doesn't have to look at me so often. But I know it breaks Mom's heart that we don't get along."

Becca shifted in her chair to look at her brother more directly. It was as if she was seeing someone she had never known before. His youthful face was haggard beyond its years. Obviously, he had not been sleeping well. "Andy, I never knew you felt this way," she said.

"We never talk about much of anything."

"Why are you talking to me now?"

"I'm not sure. Maybe because you're older now. Maybe because Christmas is coming. Maybe I don't want to be in exile anymore."

"Do you want to move back here?"

He shook his head. "I don't want to leave my job. I have a

good life in Texas. But I shouldn't have to wait until my father almost dies before I make a trip to be with my family."

Becca looked over at her father, still sleeping. The light from the hall cast a pale hue across his face. The lines in his face revealed nothing of his tortuous relationship with his son. He was a successful businessman who had provided for his family the best way he knew how. What Becca saw was a tired, ill man in his midfifties, a man that she loved. She wondered what Andy saw.

"I'm sorry, Andy," she said softly, still looking at her father.

"What for?"

"For never talking to you. For thinking Dad was right about you."

"None of that is your fault."

"Yes, it is. I'm twenty-five years old. I can form my own opinions." Becca pressed her lips together as she remembered something Andy had said early in their conversation. "Do you really think I had it easier because I was a girl?"

Andy sighed. "It sure looked that way to me. I was never the prince Dad wanted me to be, but you managed to be the princess."

"But that's ridiculous!" She almost let her voice rise too much. "Sometimes I think I don't know what it means to be serious about anything. I just sort of float along, doing whatever I feel like."

"Isn't that what a princess does?" Andy challenged. "Charm everyone and win the prizes in the end?"

Becca was silent. She thought of Dan, the prize waiting for her when she finished her adventure.

"Why did you really go to Nepal?" Andy asked.

Becca was glad the room was dark so Andy could not see her blush. "I'm discovering that my reasons for going to Nepal are more complicated than I thought. But in the beginning I went because I felt like it."

"Are you going back?"

"Yes."

"Because you feel like it?"

"Because I have to."

"What do Mom and Dad think about that?"

"I haven't discussed it with them. Of course, I'll wait until Dad is better. But I will go back."

"Good. I think you should."

"Really? I'm not sure anyone else does."

"I suppose you mean that skinny boyfriend of yours."

Becca did not respond. Andy had seen only passing glimpses of Dan, and they had never spoken, but somehow he knew exactly what Dan was thinking.

"You do what you have to do, Becca. Don't let Dan make your decisions for you."

"Do you really believe that. . .that you should do what you have to do? What if there are consequences? Look what has happened between you and Dad. You went to Texas because you thought you had to, and it didn't solve anything."

Andy was quiet for a few seconds. "I've made some choices for the wrong reasons. But basically I'm happy with my life. . . at least in Texas. It's only when I come here that I turn into somebody that even I don't like very well."

They both laughed softly.

"Andy," Becca said tentatively, "I know somebody in Nepal who might do something in order to please his parents. But I don't think he will be happy."

"Then he shouldn't do it."

"But if he doesn't do it, his family will disown him. He's not sure he wants to pay that price."

"What are you talking about, Becca?"

"They have a wife picked out for him, but he doesn't want to marry her. If he doesn't go through with it, his parents will be disgraced and never speak to him again."

"Ah, I see the problem. Has he thought about escaping to Texas? Perhaps he could share my apartment."

Becca smiled at Andy's attempt to lighten the conversation. "I'll tell him you offered," she said.

"Why don't you go home?" Andy asked.

"No, somebody has to be here all the time. That's the only way Mom will agree to get any rest."

Andy was nodding. "I know all that. I will stay."

Becca caught his eyes. "Are you sure?"

"Absolutely. I'll give the old man another chance."

"He's not old. What if he wakes up?" Becca asked, remembering Andy's earlier reluctance.

"I'll deal with it. I promise, nobody will get hurt." Andy gestured toward the door. "Get your stuff and get out of here. Grab a few hours of sleep and then make sure Mom eats a real breakfast. She looks thin to me."

Becca stuffed her mystery novel back into the backpack and leaned over to kiss her father's forehead. "If he wakes up," she said, "tell him I'll be back in the morning."

As she backed out through the doorway, Becca felt odd leaving her father and her brother alone together in the same room. That was something her family had avoided doing for as long as she could remember.

sixteen

The ringing phone jolted Becca to consciousness. Suddenly alert, she pounced on the receiver at her bedside. "Hello."

"Becca, can you come back to the hospital?" her mother's voice said calmly.

Becca stared at the numbers on her digital clock. It was almost noon. She had slept longer than she meant to. "What is it, Mom? Dad seemed fine when I left him."

"He is fine," her mother reiterated. "There is a heart available."

"What? When?"

"Just now. A young man had a car accident in Detroit. His parents have already signed the papers; the heart is on its way here."

"I'll be right there."

"Becca? Your father said Andy was here last night."

"Yes. He wanted to sit with Dad. I didn't know Dad was awake. I thought it would be all right."

"Of course it was all right. Do you know where he is now?"

Becca had a vague recollection of having heard the front door slam a couple of hours earlier.

"I'll find him, Mom."

"I suppose he doesn't have to be here."

"He'll want to be here," Becca said with confidence that she had not known the day before. "What time is the surgery scheduled for?"

"They're prepping him now. The heart should be here any minute."

"I'll be there as soon as I can." Becca hung up the phone and faced the problem of where her brother might be.

She eliminated the possibility that he would be with any of his friends, because they would all be working during the day. Andy had a knack for milling around town not doing much of anything. Becca suspected that if she just drove down the main street through town she would spot him.

His Jeep was parked outside the drugstore. Becca drove around the block looking for a parking place, and then once more. Finally, her heart pounding from anxiety, she found a place to leave her car and ran into the drugstore. Like a maniac, she rushed across the front of the store and looked down every aisle. She found him innocently looking at cold remedies. After one glance at her, he followed her unquestioningly.

They found their mother in the waiting room outside the surgical unit. "He's just gone in," she said calmly, though the color was drained from her face.

Becca winced. "I wanted to see him."

"He was already sedated when they wheeled him by here."

"Still, I would have liked to have seen him." Becca dropped into low, black vinyl chair.

"Are you all right, Mom?" Andy asked.

"Yes, of course."

"Have you eaten?"

"I had some coffee this morning."

"Let me take you down to the cafeteria and get you some lunch," Andy insisted.

"No, that's not necessary."

"Mom, you have to eat." Becca joined her brother's offensive.

"Maybe just some soup. Something hot."

"I'll go down with you," Andy said. "Becca, do you want something?"

The last thing Becca wanted to do was eat, but for her mother's sake she agreed to go to the cafeteria.

The room had a light, airy, upbeat decor that Becca found annoying. Her father was undergoing a heart transplant; why was she even noticing the maroon and blue flowers sprinkled delicately over the wallpaper? Over the loudspeaker came the tinny sound of modern renditions of Christmas carols. Becca wished she could shut it off.

They hunched together over a small pink table and perched on slate gray chairs bolted to the floor. The soup was lukewarm, but they ate it.

"How about some ice cream, Mom?" Andy offered. "Or a piece of cake?"

"Not for me, thanks, but you two go ahead." Their mother wiped the corner of her mouth with a napkin and stood up. Becca started to follow her. "Take your time," her mother said, her hand firmly on Becca's shoulder. "I'm going to go for a little walk. I'll meet you up in the waiting room."

"Are you sure you don't want us to come with you?"

"Quite sure."

"It's cold out there."

"I just need some fresh air." She left them.

Becca surveyed her brother as he absently split open a package of crackers. Against his palm, the saltines were small and fragile. "Are you okay?" she asked tentatively.

Andy did not answer.

"Did you and Dad. . .did you get a chance to talk last night?"

"I didn't want to upset him. I almost left before he woke up because I didn't want the shock to startle him."

"You're exaggerating."

"Maybe. Still, it was not really the time or place for an emotional scene."

"At least you were there with him."

Andy nodded. "He seemed to appreciate that." He split open another package of crackers, though he had not eaten the first ones.

"Did he say anything to you?"

Andy shrugged. "He was surprised to see me, and asked how long I'd been there."

"So he knows you were there all night. That must mean something to him."

"I hope so." Andy gazed into the bottom of his empty soup bowl.

Becca felt awkward, not sure of what to say next. Would Andy open up to her as he had last night? "Maybe after this operation. . . ," she started but did not know how to finish the sentence.

"I just hope he's okay."

"The doctors think he's going to be fine."

"They can't be sure. No one can be sure of anything, especially not heart transplants."

Becca reached across the table and put her hand on Andy's arm. "You'll get a chance to talk," she murmured. "You'll have a chance to put things right."

"I hope so. All these years, living in Texas, I was ready to write him off. I figured he was never going to change. But when he almost died. . .I knew I couldn't leave things that way. He's my father, after all."

Becca nodded silently.

"Let's change the subject," Andy said with sudden brightness. "How's your love life? Mom says this fellow, Dan, is quite smitten with you. Are you going to marry that rascal or not?"

"I. . .well. . .of course, we've talked about it." Now Becca reached for a package of saltines she did not want. "I have to finish my commitment in Nepal first."

"But after that?"

"I'm not sure." Becca had never spoken to Andy about anything so personal.

"Either you love him or you don't."

"It's not that black and white."

"Sure, it is."

"Love means lots of different things. Look at the way you and Dad are with each other. But you love each other. If you didn't, you'd be in Texas right now."

"Point taken, but that's not the kind of love you get married for."

"I'm not sure I know what kind of love you get married for."

"A love that you choose."

"In a lot of places, people get married for more practical reasons. Love has little to do with it."

"Like Nepal?"

She nodded.

"Like your friend? The guy you were telling me about last night?"

Becca was surprised at his insight. She had not described the specifics of the choice Barnabas faced.

"So your friend is going to marry somebody he doesn't want to marry, just to make his parents happy?" Andy probed.

"It's not that simple. You have to understand the culture, the sense of family, the obligation to honor your parents."

"If all that is true, what is holding him back?"

Becca did not answer.

"Oh," Andy said, "I get it. You. You're what's holding him back."

Becca blushed, again startled by his insight.

"So what does this mean about Dan?" Andy probed.

"I don't know." Becca was nearly squirming. "We haven't had a chance to talk things out.

"I have a feeling he's not going to like what you have to say."

Becca was silent.

Andy met Becca's eyes; his twinkled. "This is a strange conversation, isn't it?"

She smiled and sighed. "Sort of like pouring your gut out to a perfect stranger."

"Well, I'd say we're even now. You know my secret, and I know yours." He glanced at his watch. "Maybe we'd better go find Mom."

Becca mutely followed him back to the surgical waiting room.

❧

Their mother was sitting on the couch, flipping randomly through a stack of magazines. "Did you have a nice walk, Mom?" Becca asked.

"Yes, thank you. It was good to get some air. This place always smells so medicinal." She reached for another magazine.

Becca chuckled. "It is a hospital, after all."

"Yes. They play psychological games with their pretty wallpaper and pastel decor. They try to make you think you are some place pleasant. But in the end, the smell gives them away." Sarah's tone was flat from fear; she did not look at her children.

Becca sat across from her mother and picked up a magazine of her own. It was four months old, but of course she had not seen it yet.

Andy turned on the television and flipped through the afternoon talk shows and soap operas. He kept the volume low. Becca actually appreciated the background noise. It freed her to think more than she could have if the only sound were her mother's pages, jerking at random intervals.

If this operation went as well as the doctors hoped, her father would soon be on the road to recovery. The severity of his heart condition had taken everyone by surprise; her father was only fifty-four, not an old man by any means. He would take medicine for the rest of his life so that his body did not reject the heart. But he would recover.

And Becca could soon be on a plane back to Nepal, perhaps within two weeks. She could go back to her students, however reluctant some of them were. . .to Jill, her adolescent kindred spirit. . .to Barnabas. Karen had been right the other night when she said that Becca needed to see Barnabas again. She had to know what he was thinking when he put his hand against the glass in the airport. She had to tell him what she was thinking when she did the same.

She could write him a letter, but it would take so long to reach him, probably a month. She could be back in Katmandu by then. She would wait and speak to him face to face.

And what about Andy? Becca looked at him watching the television and realized he was not watching it at all. It did the same for him as it did for her. He was thinking deeply. When Becca let a magazine slap against an end table, Andy turned toward the sound.

"Sorry," she muttered and held his eyes for a moment.

Andy turned from his sister to his mother, still whipping through pages she was not reading. He hesitated for a moment, then stood up and stepped across the small room. Sitting next to his mother, he wrapped his arms around her and held her head to his shoulder. Her frantic motions stopped at last. Becca watched, choking on the lump in her throat.

A tall stranger in surgical garb appeared in the doorway and looked at Mrs. Masterson and then Becca and Andy.

"Dr. Edwards!" Her mother pulled away from Andy and was on her feet in an instant. "Is it over?"

He grinned. "Yes, and everything went beautifully. We could not have asked for a more ideal procedure. We expect a complete, routine recovery."

"Can we see him?" Becca asked.

"He hasn't come out of the anesthetic yet. He's in the recovery room. They'll move him back to cardiac intensive care when he comes around, but I expect he's going to sleep a long time."

"I understand," Becca said. "We just want to see him for ourselves."

"Of course you do. Down the hall to the left."

As their mother leaned over her unconscious husband and kissed his forehead, Andy and Becca looked at each other across the foot of the bed. A crisis had brought them together. With that behind them, they would now face their individual turning points.

seventeen

The meticulous handwriting seemed familiar, but it was out of place. Becca picked up the letter from the table inside the front door and studied the postmark: Atlanta. She did not know anyone in Atlanta. Then she recognized the writing and hastily ripped off the end of the envelope.

Dear Rebecca,

My uncle's friend is leaving for your country tonight and has agreed to carry a letter and post it to you. Harriett kindly provided your address.

I have prayed much for your father. The Lord has given me a peace about his recovery. I am confident that by the time this letter reaches you, a weight will have been lifted off your heart. Please greet your father for me in the name of Jesus.

I am sorry that we did not get a chance to talk before you left Katmandu. Only at the last minute did I hear about your father's illness and your trip home. There is much I would like to share with you. Time does not permit a lengthy letter, so I must simply assure you of my prayers and friendship.

I hope this reaches you before Christmas, so we can give thanks for the birth of our Lord together.

With every hope of seeing you soon,

Barnabas

Becca tried to swallow the lump in her throat but it refused to go down. While she had debated about writing to Barnabas, she had not expected to hear from him.

Her father was indeed much better. Ten days had passed since the surgery, and he had shown no sign of complications. He was alert most of the day, engaged in mild physical therapy, and would soon be discharged.

Becca had already inquired with a travel agent about flights to Katmandu soon after Christmas. Her mother seemed vaguely distressed that she was leaving again but spoke no words to dissuade Becca. Her father was glad for every moment they spent together, but he, too, knew that she would go soon. Andy had already gone back to Texas. Life would return to normal.

And then there was Dan. Becca had not seen much of him, actually not nearly as much as she expected to, once her father was past the crisis. She had supposed that after the surgery she would be able to relax with Dan as she had in the past, and in that context she would search her soul for signs about the future of their relationship. God would make clear to her whether she should marry him or not.

But the truth was that she had not really missed Dan. Perhaps that in itself was an indication of her true feelings. The sensible thing to do was to finish her term in Nepal and come back to marry Dan and resume teaching school in a conventional classroom. She was an American; she understood American culture. She would fit in here as she would never fit in overseas. But could she be content with that, now that she had seen how much of the rest of the world lives?

She thought of Jill, thirteen years old but longing to do something significant with her life, to make her own choice about how or where she would serve God. Though straining to be an adult, Jill was a child; her decisions were limited by the discernment of her parents. But Becca was twice Jill's age, and her choices were her own. She had seen that more clearly in the last six months then in the whole rest of her life.

Barnabas also faced a choice, and although he was an adult, older than Becca even, he met with constraints. Whatever choice he made, he would pay dearly for it.

Part of Becca wished she could simply slip out of the country and be on her way. But she knew she would have to make her peace with Dan before she left. And Dan would arrive shortly to take her to dinner.

Tucking the letter inside her purse, she went upstairs and dressed for an evening out. Thirty minutes later, Dan rang the bell, ready to escort her for the evening.

He chose a restaurant he knew Becca liked. The high-backed wooden booths created a sense of solitude, of separation from the world. The only intrusion was the occasional quiet attention of the waiter. Between them on the table, a candle glowed, speckling the table top with mysterious shadows. The meal was northern Italian cuisine: a generous salad, garlic bread, meat-stuffed pasta with a mouth-watering white cheese sauce. The atmosphere was perfect. Becca was suspicious. They talked through most of the meal. Dan seemed nervous, which made Becca even more suspicious.

Over a triple-layer, double-chocolate fudge cake, Dan said, "Becca, I have something for you."

"A Christmas present?" Becca's heart sank. She had been so preoccupied with her father's health that Christmas shopping for Dan had never entered her mind.

"Not exactly. It's something I've been wanting to give you for a long time."

Her heart pounded. Surely he had not gone out and bought a diamond ring! She had given him no reason to believe she would accept one at this point in time.

But instead of reaching into a small pocket, as she had imagined he would, Dan reached for a folder on the bench beside him. He laid it on the table where she could see it plainly in the light of the candle and opened it. "Merry Christmas," he said.

"Real estate brochures?" she asked quizzically.

He nodded enthusiastically. "It's a new subdivision on the south edge of town. They have some great starter houses there."

"Starter houses?" She raised her eyebrows.

"Yes. I walked through several of them last week, and one of them would be perfect for us."

"Dan, what are you talking about?"

"I put money down on a house." He slid the brochures to one side to reveal a photograph of a split-level suburban home. "It'll be ready in about six weeks."

Becca nearly dropped her fork. "You put money down on a house? I didn't know you were thinking of buying a house."

"It's always been in my plans to buy a house. Lots of couples have to scrape and save to come up with a down payment, but we don't have to go through that. I've saved enough already. I know six weeks is not enough time to plan a wedding, but we could go ahead and start decorating together."

Becca set her fork down solidly. "What are you talking about, Dan? If you want to buy a house, that's great. I'm sure it's a great investment. But I'm going back to Nepal right after Christmas. I never said anything about getting married."

"We've talked about it dozens of times."

"But we never decided anything. . .at least, I didn't. It appears that you have."

Dan closed the folder abruptly. "You've been under a lot of stress since you came home. I wanted to do something for you. I thought the idea of a house would bring you pleasure."

Becca forced herself to stay calm. "Dan, you can't make my decisions for me. I've said all along that I was going to go back to Nepal and finish my commitment there before deciding on anything else."

"Okay. I give up. You're going back to Nepal. I accept that.

But only for a few months. We could get engaged now and get married when you get back."

Becca looked into Dan's dark eyes. She saw no pleading or longing, simply control. He was determined to make this decision. "No, Dan," she finally said.

He was silent and pressed his lips together.

"I don't think we should get married," Becca said. "I had my doubts when I left the first time, and then I thought that it was only because I was away from you that I was doubting. But I don't think so. We just don't want the same things."

"That's trite," Dan said sharply.

"But it's true."

"What happened to you, Becca? I thought after your father's crisis was over we'd go back to the way we were."

"I don't think we can. The kind of life you want. . .I'm not sure I want that now."

Dan tapped the folder. "You don't want to live in a house? Do you want to spend the rest of your life in a hut without electricity?"

"A year ago that house would have been really tempting," she conceded. "But not anymore."

"What's different now?"

"I'm different."

"You're jetlagged."

"I got over that a long time ago." She was getting tired of his pointed tone and she worked hard to stay calm.

"Then you are in some kind of culture shock. I've read stuff about that. I understand that your mind is somewhere else because of this commitment you made. But you have less than six months left. Then what?"

"I'm not sure."

"You have to think about the long term, Becca. You'll come back to the States and pick up your life."

"Maybe, maybe not."

"What are you saying?" Dan was visibly impatient.

"I'm saying that I haven't made up my mind about what I'll do when my term is finished."

"You're not seriously thinking about staying in Nepal?" he asked, incredulous.

"I haven't decided anything. I'm not the same person I was when I left, and I don't know how much more I'll change after I get back to Nepal."

"You were a fine person before you left," Dan said. "An excellent teacher, wonderful to your parents, you have good friends who care about you. . .your life is here, Becca."

"Your life is here, Dan," she retorted. "You can say that with certainty. You can't say anything about my life. I have to decide that. I have to know what my life means."

"I don't think that question was foremost in your mind when you flew off to the other side of the world."

"No, it wasn't," she admitted. "I was being impetuous when I left. But God can use even foolish decisions. He's doing something inside me, despite my own resistance."

"So now this is some kind of spiritual experience?" Dan's tone was mocking and unconvinced.

"Why is that so hard to believe?"

"You've never been that kind of a Christian."

"What kind of Christian?"

"The kind that talks about the Will of God in every little thing."

"Maybe I never had to be. Maybe my life has been too comfortable. Maybe I never really had to make a decision on my own before."

"Having electricity and running water does not make a person unspiritual."

"That's not what I'm talking about, and you know it," Becca admonished. "Dan, I'm being stretched in ways I never thought about before. And I like it. I can't say I'll marry you when I'm not who you think I am."

"Well, I'm quite fond of the old you. Surely she's in there somewhere."

"Maybe she is, but she'll never be the same.

Dan was silent.

"I'll miss you, Dan," Becca said with finality.

The waiter appeared with their bill.

eighteen

Becca stuffed her carry-on bag—considerably fuller than when she came home a few weeks ago—into the overhead compartment and sank into the aisle seat below it. The last couple of weeks were a blur and her head was still spinning.

Her father had come home from the hospital; a home health care nurse checked on him every day; Becca and her mother were satisfied that he was going to be fine. The color in his face was more normal each day, and although he had had to make some adjustments in his eating habits, his appetite was good and he was regaining some of the weight he had lost while in the hospital.

Andy had stayed for Christmas, although he had resumed working by getting out his laptop computer and establishing phone contact with his office in Texas several times a day. He had carved out a corner of the living room to use as working space; the television had stayed off for days at a stretch. Watching him, Becca had seen a dimension she had not known before; he spoke with confidence and authority when he was one the phone; he kept his desktop neat and organized, with his list of tasks to complete always handy. Clearly he was good at what he did, though Becca understood little about the insurance industry.

For the first time since she was in high school, her whole family sat down to Christmas dinner together and actually conversed in friendly tones. Andy never told Becca what he had talked about with their father in the hospital, but she could see the change in their relationship. While the peace was still fragile, the old tension was gone and they looked for opportunities to be in the same room together. And despite the stress of her husband's illness, Sarah Masterson had acquired an inner quiet that Becca had not seen in years.

Right after Christmas, Andy had gone back to Texas with plans to return in the summer. Becca was booked on a flight before New Year's.

Now, sitting on the airplane, she looked out at the frosty view and tried to breathe away the heavy feeling in her chest. It was harder to leave her parents than she had thought it would be. She wanted to go back to Nepal; she had not recanted. But the crisis—and the emotional turning point—in her family weighed on her mind.

She had not seen Dan since their breakup. When the emotion of their last evening together had worn off, she was left with relief that she had finally taken her stand with Dan. She understood the freedom Andy had gained by taking a stand with their father; she, too, was ready to move beyond habits and presumptions and look to the future. And now here she sat, on a plane headed across the Pacific Ocean once again.

"I guess that's my seat."

Becca turned her head away from the window and toward the voice. A young woman in a denim miniskirt and a thin tee shirt with a scooped neckline tossed a canvas backpack over Becca's head and into the window seat. Becca scrunched up her knees to let the woman pass. Heavy perfume hung in the air, nearly making Becca gag. The woman stuffed her backpack under the seat in front of her and plopped her scrawny hips down into the seat. Her tight skirt rose well up on her thighs. She swept her wavy red hair, darker at the roots, away from her face, her multiple bracelets dangling with the motion.

Becca inwardly shrank from interaction with her seatmate, turning her attention to a magazine in her lap.

"First time to Asia?" the woman asked, foiling Becca's effort at isolation.

"Uh, no, actually I was in Nepal for about six months."

"Going back there?"

"Yes."

"Trekking?"

"Teaching, actually."

"Yeah? Cool." The woman snapped her gum. "In an American school?"

"Sort of. I have a one-room school for American children whose parents are working in one of the mountain villages." She did not mention that the parents were all missionaries.

"Is this like a career thing? Is that why you're going back?"

"I'm. . .not sure. Um, it's just a one-year contract right now." Becca wanted to change the subject, so she said, "How about you?"

"Tokyo."

"Vacation?" Becca had a difficult time picturing this woman in a proper Japanese setting.

"Yep. I like to travel."

"Have you been there before?"

"Nah. I never go the same place twice. I've been to seventeen different countries in the last five years."

"Oh, I see."

"Too much to do and see to stay in one place."

Becca nodded.

"Well, I haven't slept in two days, what with the goodbye parties and all. I'm gonna crash. Wake me when the cocktails come, okay?"

Almost instantly, the woman was asleep. Becca found herselt staring at this strangely restful creature beside her, so different from herself. Here was someone to whom life was a constant adventure. But did she know what it was like to make a commitment? But then, did Becca? She was not so sure.

Since receiving Barnabas's note, Becca had tried at least three times to write to him. But the words never looked right on the paper and she had crumpled up each of the letters. What could she say? That she had broken up with Dan, so she could marry him now? That seemed presumptuous. What if he no longer wanted her? Besides, she was not sure she was ready to say she could marry him, even apart from Dan. Marrying Barnabas and living in Nepal would be an enormous commitment. She was not sure she was strong enough to make it.

Becca looked at the woman sleeping next to her. Maybe they were not so different after all.

❧

Twenty-four hours later, the mission guest house in Katmandu was a welcome sight. Becca paid the taxi driver, watched him maneuver around the pothole in front of the gate, and turned to face the house. The back door opened and Harriett stuck her head out.

"I wish you had let me meet you at the airport," the older woman said.

Becca smiled wanly. "Thanks, but I needed to do something to force me to use the language. I got here fine."

"But you're exhausted. I can see that." Harriett held the door open and Becca stepped into the rear of the dining room. The familiar worn couches and bookcases were still there and some of the same magazines. Harriett persisted. "When did you eat last?"

Becca shrugged. "It's hard to keep track of time on an airplane. I think it was about six hours ago."

"Then you must eat now." Harriett was not asking a question this time. She pointed at a chair. "Sit there. I will bring you a sandwich."

"What, no rice and curry?" Becca asked, smiling.

"We'll give you one more day to work up to that." Harriett disappeared into the kitchen where the Nepali cook was already scrubbing vegetables for the evening meal.

Becca obediently sat in the designated chair and she looked

around the room. Everything was the same. The throw pillows were slightly more faded than six months ago, and someone had rearranged the paperbacks in the bookcase. But the mission house stood firm, a reliable refuge for those who passed through it. Becca was glad for the buffer zone and a few days to reacclimate herself before going back to the village. Unless the flight schedule changed, she would have four days before continuing her journey.

By the time Harriett returned with a sandwich and glass of reconstituted powdered milk, Becca had decided that she was hungry. She ate heartily, while reporting on her father's improved health. Then she was ready for Harriett to lead the way to her assigned room, where the power of jetlag overshadowed her will to stay awake. She was soon deeply asleep.

She woke abruptly and, disoriented by the strange, darkened room, floundered and stubbed her toe when she got out of bed. Why was it so dark? Surely she had not slept the entire day. She stumbled toward the window and raised the shade, relieved to find the afternoon sun still shining brightly. Squinting at her watch, she realized she had slept four hours. A dream had awakened her, but now she could not say what it had been about. She rubbed her eyes. Barnabas had been in the dream, she knew that much. But why had she wakened with such a frightened sensation?

She glanced at her watch again. If the language school were in session, Barnabas would be there now. She did not even know if he knew she was in Katmandu. Harriett was the only missionary she had communicated with, but Becca did not know whether Harriett saw Barnabas very often. She suspected not.

Becca looked in the mirror and groaned. Vainly, she patted her cheeks and tried to smooth down her hair. She did not want Barnabas to see her like this. Without realizing it, she had decided to go find him. First she would have to find the shower and some fresh clothing.

❧

"*Namaste!*" Becca greeted the guard at the gate outside the language school. He remembered her and cheerfully allowed her to pass. With slow steps she walked into the main courtyard, feeling the weight of memories pulsing through her. Her life had taken an unexpected turn in this place and had found a path that would never lead back to the old days. But where would it lead?

A rack of bicycles and motorcycles told Becca that class was in session. At the end of the row was the motorcycle Barnabas used for slithering through the narrow streets of Katmandu. Becca's mind clouded over as her heart quickened. What was she going to say to him. She wished she had at least acknowledged his letter more than a month ago. Now she felt as if she had no starting point with him.

Becca's feet took her along the familiar path past the dining room to the building where the language sessions were held. Through an open window, Patricia's voice rose and fell on the breeze, giving Becca a rapid refresher course on common verbs. Parking herself on the stone steps outside the building, Becca could not help but listen to the instructor's intonations of the verbs, and she began repeating them back along with the unseen class. After a few minutes, the scraping of chairs on the wooden floor told her that the students were working with their tutors for the last few minutes of the day.

Becca pictured herself inside the classroom, huddled over a textbook with Barnabas, listening with untrained ears to his pronunciation of the scratchlike symbols on the patch. During the first week of the course, she had been convinced she could never learn to speak Nepali. The written squiggles just did not make sense, and her ears simply did not hear the subtle distinctions in sound that formed individual words. But Barnabas had been extraordinarily patient, far beyond her own capacity, and the language had taken shape in her mind. By the time she flew back to the States, she was far from fluent, but she was no longer terrified that a shopkeeper or taxi driver might speak to her.

Squinting into the sun, Becca smiled at the analogy drifting through her mind. Could Barnabas be as patient with her while she sorted out her emotions and ability to make a commitment? And would she eventually be less terrified by the pull she now felt on her life?

A door opened behind her. Class was over. Students and tutors, books tucked under their arms, spilled out and spread across the courtyard in pairs and small groups. Becca knew most of the tutors and greeted them enthusiastically in Nepali, all the while looking for the one tutor she had come to see. When the others had finished chatting and moved on, Barnabas still had not appeared. Becca tentatively moved into the classroom. Barnabas, characteristically, had remained to help straighten up. Barely breathing, Becca watched his simple, smooth motions as he lined up a dozen chairs. His conversation with Patricia was sparse and muted. He did not see Becca standing in the doorway but Patricia did.

"Miss Masterson! What are you doing here?"

Becca blushed. This was not the reunion she had imagined. She watched as Barnabas turned around and met her eyes.

"I. . .just got back to Katmandu. . .I was in the States. . .my father was ill." Being polite to Patricia was difficult when what she really wanted was to talk to Barnabas.

"So I heard," Patricia said, glancing at Barnabas. "Well, I think we're finished here. Stop by again if you have a chance." And she was gone.

"Hi," Becca said to Barnabas, nervously.

"Hello, Rebecca. I am very glad to see you are well."

"I. . .didn't know if anyone told you I was coming."

He shook his head. "No. I have not spoken to any of the missionaries lately."

She sighed. "I got your letter. Thank you. I'm sorry I didn't answer."

"It does not matter. Your father was ill and you had many things on your mind."

"Well. . .yes." His assessment was true, even if not complete.

"Your father is. . .?"

"Oh, he's fine," Becca quickly explained. "He had a heart transplant. The doctors are very encouraged."

Barnabas shook his head. "I am always amazed at such things."

"Me, too. But thankful."

"Yes. God is good."

"And your family?"

"They are fine. My mother is quite happy."

"Oh?"

"She is happy. . .because of the wedding."

Becca's heart nearly stopped. "The wedding?" she echoed weakly. "Have you. . .?"

"I have agreed to the bride my parents have chosen.

"Oh." The color drained from her face. "I. . .I. . ."

"I must become a pilot, Rebecca," he explained insistently. "It is the only way to get the Gospel to the far villages."

"But—"

"The wedding is not for another year. The girl still wants to wait. And then we will go to the States, away from the strength of the Hindu culture. I am trusting that God will bring His light to the heart of my wife."

"Yes, of course."

"I hope you will join me in praying for this."

"Certainly. I want you to be happy, and I know how much you want to serve the Lord."

They were silent, still standing ten feet apart. Barnabas slowly moved toward her. "I did not know if you were even coming back," he said.

"That's my fault. I'm sorry."

"But I'm glad you are here."

"I still have six months left on my commitment to the children."

"They have missed you, especially Jill."

"And I've missed them."

"I hope we will be able to see each other."

"Will you be in my village?"

He nodded.

Becca fought to keep back the tears, but her eyes misted over. Even through her tears, though, she was sure she saw tears in his eyes, too.

nineteen

The breeze rifled the yellow chintz curtain on the open window and blew across Becca's desk. Instinctively, she reached for the loose papers to keep them from scattering and she then set a stapler on top of the pile. She glanced up at her students, hard at work on their math assignments. Mandy Bridgman's feet were thumping rhythmically against her chair's legs, her characteristic signal that she was about to reach the end of her attention span. Tommy was chewing his pencil, stumped; word problems were hard for him. Lizzie was doodling, probably because she was already finished. Becca was comforted to see that the traits in her students had not changed during her absence. She still knew them well enough to adjust assignments to their individual needs as much as possible.

In the two weeks since she had returned to the village, Becca had been absorbed with the challenge of returning to teaching. The missionaries had done their best to keep school going while she was gone, but now Becca had to determine how much progress the children had made. Without actually saying she was giving a test, she had done that in nearly every subject. When they turned in the math worksheets they were doing now, she would have all the information she needed to begin planning for the coming weeks.

She glanced at the clock and said, "Time is up. If you didn't finish, don't worry. You can finish another time. Enjoy the afternoon and I'll see you all back here in the morning."

The children offered no resistance and quickly cleared out of the back-porch classroom. Only Jill remained; Becca had promised her they could talk about the reading program. Becca was quite curious about it, actually, and sorry that she had not had time for Jill sooner.

Becca quickly picked up the math assignments and added them to the pile under the stapler. Then she turned her attention to Jill.

"Finally!" she said enthusiastically. "I've been so anxious to hear how the reading class is doing." She sat down at a desk next to Jill, who had reached into her own desk and pulled out a folder of papers.

"I wish I had more to tell you," Jill said. "But I've been a little discouraged."

"Why?"

Jill shrugged. "Some of the girls don't come all the time anymore. They say their mothers need them."

"Unfortunately, they probably do."

"I'm not so sure. I think their mothers stopped letting them come because there was not a real teacher here while you were gone."

"What do you mean?" Becca asked, surprised. "You were always the one who was teaching the girls."

"I know. But they all knew you were helping me plan. With you gone. . ."

"Well, I'm sorry about that, but we'll just have to figure out a way to get back on track." She leaned toward Jill's desk. "Show me what you worked on while I was gone."

For the next ninety minutes, they bent their heads over the desk and shuffled papers around. Jill gave a status report on each of the students, and together they worked out lesson plans for the next couple of weeks.

"You're doing beautifully, Jill," Becca said, squeezing the girl's shoulder. "I'm really proud of you."

Jill blushed. "Thanks. I'm pretty proud of myself, I guess."

"You should be." Becca stood up, thinking that their work was done.

Jill started to say something, then hesitated.

"What is it?" Becca asked.

"Well. . .it's not really my business. . .I've just been wondering about something."

"You can ask me. If I don't want to answer, I'll tell you."

"It's not about you exactly, but maybe you know the answer." Jill took a deep breath and plunged ahead. "I heard my parents talking about Barnabas. They said that he decided to get married, and that he's going to marry a Hindu. Is that true?"

Becca coughed gently to disguise a gasp. "Yes, it is true," she finally said.

"But how can he do that? I can't believe it's what he wants."

Becca chose her words carefully, trying to be objective and not caught up in her own emotions about the situation. "Barnabas is in a tough spot," Becca said. "He wants to honor his parents; it's an important part of his culture."

"But all the missionaries say that Barnabas is one of the most talented, Christian Nepali leaders. How can he have a Hindu wife?"

"It's very complicated, Jill. You know Barnabas well enough to know that he wants to bring glory to God with his life more than anything else."

"That's why I don't understand—"

"If he marries, his parents will help him become a pilot."

"I know he wants to be able to fly to the villages. . .but with a Hindu wife? It just doesn't make sense."

"It's his choice. We have to trust Barnabas to make the best decision he can, considering his limited options." Becca struggled to make Barnabas's decision sound credible, even though she had many of the same questions that Jill expressed.

"He doesn't have to marry this woman just because his parents want him to!"

"Jill, you and I are Americans, and we have a lot of freedom of choice. You've been in Nepal most of your life. Surely you can see that the culture is different here. We can't possibly understand the dilemma he faces."

Jill sighed. "I guess not. But this just can't be right. Maybe Barnabas is giving up on God too soon."

Becca did not respond. The same question rattled her own mind, but she had found no answer in nearly two weeks of fitful nights.

"Dad said Barnabas is coming to dinner tonight," Jill said.

"Yes, he told me, too."

"Are you going to talk to him?"

"What do you mean?"

"Well, before you left. . .I thought. . .well, you know."

How could Becca give Jill an answer she did not have herself? "I know what you're getting at," Becca said, "but that's one of those questions I just can't answer for you."

Jill gathered up her things. "If you're not going to talk to him, maybe I will."

Becca smiled slightly at the girl's tenacity. "Let's just take one thing at a time," she said softly.

Jill left then and Becca was alone in the classroom. It was here that she had come for refuge nearly every evening during the last two weeks, staying and working as long as she could without stirring up probing questions from onlookers. Her attempts to exhaust herself with work brought mixed results. Physically, she was tired, but her emotional distress was undimmed. Slipping into bed each night brought no relief. Hardly a dark hour passed that she did not see Barnabas's face rise up before her, mournful and resigned instead of joyful and content. In her dreams, she ran toward him, clutching him close only to have him disappear from her arms before she could tell him she loved him. . .for she did love him.

❧

Two hours later, Becca sat across the table from Barnabas and took the hands of two of the Bridgman children while their father gave thanks for the food. As the rice bowl was passed around, she caught Barnabas's eye and smiled as genuinely as she could. In response, the color drained from his face and he avoided looking directly at her again, although he included her in his conversation.

The meal was finally over. "We'll clean up," David Bridgman said. "You two need a chance to catch up with each other."

A split second of awkwardness passed as Becca heard Barnabas say, "Thank you. I was hoping Rebecca and I would have an opportunity for one of our walks."

She was glad for the dim lighting as her face flushed.

They walked out to the edge of the village. The night was moonless, so they dared not venture farther down the potholed path. Instead, they sat on a familar chunk of fallen wood in a clearing where they knew they could see the stars above the mountain trees. Barnabas sat down first, in the middle of the short log. Becca discreetly sat down next to him, overwhelmed by his nearness. For days she had practiced various versions of what she would say when they met again. She had so much to say and so much to ask; none of her imagined scripts seemed right. She needed more time to read his mood, she decided, time for him to give her some signal about why he was eager to take a walk together. Becca did not say anything.

" 'The heavens declare the glory of God; and the firmament sheweth his handywork,' " Barnabas quoted Psalm 19:1.

Becca followed his gaze to the jeweled blackness above them. "Where I come from," she said, "the sky does not look like this. I had to come to Nepal to understand that verse. The sky is a mystery I will never comprehend."

"One mystery among others."

Becca looked over at Barnabas, his face still pointed upward. "What do you mean?"

"It is also a mystery how the Creator of those stars should

work His way in my life. . .and yours." He turned toward her, unexpectedly changing the subject. "Tell me the news of your family."

The shift caught Becca off guard. "Well, my dad will have to take medication the rest of his life, but the doctors think he will be fine. We're all relieved and grateful, even Andy."

"Andy?"

"My brother."

"But you never told me you had a brother!" Barnabas was genuinely surprised.

"Sorry. He lives in another part of the country, and we don't see him very often. Actually, he and my father haven't gotten along too well. . .until now." Becca found herself giving Barnabas a full account of what had transpired between her brother and father over the last fifteen years.

"How sad those years must have been for all of you," was his response, "and how glad you must be that they have reconciled."

"Yes," Becca answered simply. She took a deep breath. "But the experience has taught me something. I have an idea of the pain you would feel if you could not be with your family. I know how important that is to you. . .even more than it was to Andy." She choked on her words. "So I guess I understand the decision that you made. It is a choice that requires great faith, but God has prepared you. We can't always understand His leading, but He will honor your faithfulness. One day we will look back and it will all make sense. In the meantime, I will join you in your prayers for your wife."

Barnabas chuckled quietly.

"What is it?" Becca asked urgently, suddenly flustered.

"Forgive me, but how long have you been practicing that speech?"

She looked away. "Sorry. I just wasn't sure what I should say to you."

"The words are not important, Rebecca. The question is, do you believe them?"

"I want to," she whispered, as much to herself as to him.

They sat in silence, once again staring at the stars.

twenty

Becca snuggled into her bed more out of habit than readiness to sleep. She had not slept well since returning to the village, and on this night she was especially wakeful. It was not emotional stress that kept her awake, but emotional energy. The moments with Barnabas on the log, looking at the stars had stirred her up rather than settled her down. Becca had expected that their conversation would bring finality to their previous relationship. From now on they would be occasional co-workers, and in a few months, Becca would go home to the States.

But that had not happened. Instead of words bringing closure, the unspoken thoughts between them—and Barnabas's last question— broke open Becca's mind and heart. Now, lying in the dark in her tiny room, she knew she did not believe the little speech she had made. If she herself had not been so indecisive a few weeks ago, Barnabas would not be in the corner he was in now. He had come to her in this very village with a clear conviction that God wanted them to be together, and she had cast doubt on his belief, using Dan as the excuse. Now what was her excuse? Her own fear was all that stood in the path, keeping them apart. The fear was real; the challenge of living her life in Nepal had not changed. Something inside her had changed, though. Was it too late to act on new convictions?

Becca swung her legs over the side of the bed and groped on the nightstand for the matches. She lit the candle and stared into its flame, the only thing rupturing the solid darkness. But the tiny flame was all that was needed to change the appearance of the room. Its flickering lightened Becca's heart with hope.

She would not give up without a fight, she determined. Barnabas was leaving early in the morning, but she would catch him at the first light.

❧

When the dawn finally broke, Becca dressed quickly and went outside. Barnabas was crossing the compound. "We have to talk, Barnabas," she blurted out, more abruptly than she intended."

"Good morning, Rebecca," was his calm reply. He was on his way for breakfast. "Are you hungry?"

She put a hand on his arm. "Breakfast can wait. Let's go back out to our log."

Meekly, he followed her back out to the edge of the village and sat beside her. His face was a puzzle, but she focused on what she wanted to say, not on trying to second-guess his thoughts.

"You were right. Last night. I don't believe what I said. Well, parts of it, maybe. I know God has been preparing you and He will honor your faithfulness. But not the part about understanding your decision."

"Rebecca—"

She continued, oblivious to the interruption. "It's all my fault that you have decided to marry a Hindu woman."

"I made the choice."

"But you asked me, weeks ago, to marry you. You were prepared to take the consequences, even if your family did not approve. And I walked away without giving you an honest explanation."

"But your young man. . . ? You said there was someone waiting for you at home."

"That's what I said, and I suppose it was true. He was waiting for me. But I think I already knew I did not want to go back to him. I was afraid."

"Afraid?"

"Of what people would think if we were married, of living in a strange culture the rest of my life, of having the kind of faith that you have."

"Rebecca, what are you saying?"

"I should have said 'yes.' And I want to say 'yes' now, if you'll let me."

His eyes widened. "You mean. . .get married?"

She nodded somberly. "I've caused you a lot of pain by not telling you the truth earlier. And if I had only written to you from the States you might not have given in to your parents. I'm sorry for all that. But I know what I want now. And I'm not afraid of being afraid."

"Rebecca, I am not sure what to say."

"I know, I know. I've made things very complicated, haven't I? Now you are engaged. You have given your word. What gives me the right to ask you to break your word? But that is what I am asking you to do, because I don't believe you gave your heart."

He looked down at the ground quietly. "You are correct."

Becca stood up and began shuffling around in the dirt. Now that her outburst was over, nervousness overwhelmed her. What was he going to say?

He looked up at Becca, who was starting to pace, and then looked away again. "It is true that I did not give my heart to the girl, but I gave my word to my mother. A few months ago she would have accepted that I did not wish to marry the girl she has chosen. But to take back my promise now. . .I gave my word."

"But I thought the engagement was not public yet. Will she

be dishonored if no one knows?"

"I will dishonor her with my action. And the girl's parents will believe I do not think their daughter is worthy."

Becca slumped onto the log beside Barnabas. "I have hurt so many people with my own confusion. Why couldn't I see things this clearly two months ago?"

Barnabas was silent, thinking deeply.

"The last thing I want to do," continued Becca, "is hurt the feelings of a teen-age girl I don't even know. Or your mother . . .I want to love her as you do. But we must find a way, Barnabas."

He glanced at his watch. "I must begin my hike," he said distantly. He stood up.

"Barnabas?"

"I will visit my parents this weekend," he said. "Then I will send word to you. I cannot leave my student again, so I will not be back here for six weeks or more."

"Six weeks?"

"But I will send word." A few minutes later, Barnabas was gone, without his breakfast.

❧

Waiting was torture. Becca told no one of her final conversation with Barnabas. This meant that she had to function as normally as possible while she waited to hear from him. He had left the village on a Wednesday, intending to see his family on the following weekend. Then he would have to get back to Katmandu to send a message on the radio or a letter by plane. A radio message would be faster; a letter would be private. Becca knew he would choose to be private.

The days crawled by and the nights were interminable. Becca nodded absently at almost anything her students asked her, daydreamed her way through meals with the missionary families, and wrote letters to her friend, Karen, that she never mailed.

One day she gave the children the afternoon off for no reason at all except that she could not concentrate on a thing they were saying. David Bridgman asked if something was bothering her, but she did not confide.

Repeatedly, Becca chastised herself for not waiting with more contentment. Why could she not rest peacefully as God's will was worked out? Because, in a place deep inside her, she was afraid she had missed her opportunity for happiness by not recognizing it the first time it appeared.

On the morning of the ninth day, the plane came in with the mailbag. Becca had several letters, all from the States. She stood in the Bridgman kitchen, masking her disappointment. She looked from David to Sandy and back again, weighing in her mind how much she trusted them. Finally, she blurted out, "I have to go to Katmandu." She startled them both. Obviously they needed more explanation, but she was hesitant to give it.

"I need to see Barnabas. It's important."

"Is something wrong?" David asked gently.

"I'm not sure. That's what I have to find out." She looked urgently at him. "Do you think there is any space on the plane this afternoon?"

"Oh, Becca, I don't know. Unless it's an emergency—"

She shook her head. "No, no, it's not an emergency. But it is important."

"I knew something was bothering you lately," Sandy said. "You haven't been the same since you came back."

"Please, I can't explain right now. Can you help me get a seat on the plane?"

David looked at his watch. "Put on your hiking shoes. We'll got down to the landing strip and I'll see what I can do."

❧

Four hours later, Becca landed in Katmandu and hailed a cab to take her to the language school. This time she did not make herself wait on the steps outside; she stood in the doorway of the classroom, watching him work. Holding still to avoid creating a disturbance, she studied his movements and expressions. He seemed peaceful, serene—the old Barnabas she had admired before her trip home. Whatever decision he had come to—with its consequences—he had found restored contentment. For that, Becca was glad.

Class was soon over, and Becca made her presence known. Smiling graciously at the others she knew in the room, she pulled Barnabas aside.

"Rebecca! What are you doing here?"

"I couldn't wait any longer. I had to come."

He tapped a letter in his shirt pocket. "I wrote to you, but I missed the pickup for the mail run."

"That doesn't matter now. Can we go somewhere to talk?"

They settled on a bench in the garden courtyard of the former palace.

"We can begin to plan our wedding," he said simply and brightly.

She lit up. "Your family?"

"No, they will not attend." He looked off into the distance and spoke wistfully. "My mother reacted as I thought she would and my father is angry that I hurt my mother. I don't know if I can ever go home again."

"Oh, Barnabas, I'm so sorry. It grieves me to come between you and your family."

He shook his head. "No, you have not done that. You gave me courage to do what I should have done, anyway. I was trying to chart my own course. It is better if I take the course God charts, even if it takes a little longer to become a pilot."

"We'll figure something out," Becca said. "Teachers don't

make a lot of money by American standards, but we won't need much. There should be something left for school fees."

He looked at her, wide eyed. "You would do that for me?"

"Of course. We'll save for as long as it takes. Keep that letter of acceptance handy."

She still saw a look of disbelief in his eyes. Suddenly not caring what anyone thought, she threw her arms around him. "I love you, Barnabas," she whispered in his ear.

When she pulled back to look at his face, she saw tears in his eyes.

twenty-one

The weeks stopped crawling and started walking, even running sometimes. Becca stayed only a few days in Katmandu before she had to return to the village and her classroom. The fear that Barnabas would turn her away in order to honor his mother was gone, and in its place was the overwhelming task of getting ready for what lay ahead of them. Before she even left Katmandu, Becca posted a letter to her old principal, asking advice for finding a job for the next school year. She could not go back to Porter. She would have to find a teaching position near the training program Barnabas had been accepted into and that meant she would have to get certification in another state. Everything she and Barnabas wanted to do would hinge on Becca's getting a job that she could begin almost as soon as she arrived home.

The answer came back in less than a month. Her former principal had an friend from college who was a superintendent in the area where Becca wanted to go. She included a list of addresses of districts with openings and Becca fired off letters as quickly as she could, painfully aware that the recipients might not sympathize with the need for handwritten correspondence from Nepal.

Applying from halfway around the world, she knew, was not in her favor. She was not available for interviews, and since she had quit her job, she had lost her modest seniority in her own district. She was starting all over again. Mentally, she worked on a budget. They would have to be frugal, and Barnabas might have to find a part-time job, but they could scrape by if she could just get a teaching job.

The missionaries, for the most part, had accepted the news of her engagement with enthusiasm. A few had their reservations because of her short time in Nepal. They were not convinced she knew what she was committing herself to. But the others were so pleased that Barnabas would have a Christian wife after all that they glossed over the difficulties Becca might face.

The news from home was mixed. Becca had sent letters to her parents, Andy, and Karen all in the same day, and got back responses in the same batch of mail.

"I saw it coming," Karen wrote. "Of course you were stressed out about your dad while you were home, but I knew it was more than that. Your mind—and heart—were somewhere else. This guy better be good to deserve you. I'm looking forward to meeting him. I promise that my interrogation will be gentle." Becca had known all along that Karen would support whatever choice she made.

Andy's letter was exuberant. "Hooray! Is this the mysterious friend we talked about in the hospital that night? Guess he won't be needing to share my apartment after all! Name the day, and I'll be there."

Her mother's letter conveyed stiff thoughts in soft words. "Becca, of course we want you to be happy, and we do trust your ability to make your own decisions. It's just that you have been experiencing so much change in the last few months, added to the stress of your father's illness. We wonder if this is the time to make such an enormous decision as getting married to someone like this young man and pledging to live in his country. I see Dan around town from time to time. I'm sure he would be delighted to hear from you."

At first, Becca had been angry at her parents' reaction. Did they really think she would change her mind because they waved

Dan in front of her face like a carrot before a horse? Barnabas had written that she should try to understand their perspective, and she had calmed down enough to realize that they were just suspicious of something unfamiliar. As soon as they met Barnabas, they would see that he was the perfect choice for her, no matter what culture he came from. She had overlooked the underlying tone of the letter and had written back, asking her mother to check the church calendar for a wedding date.

Her mother's letter was the first time Becca came face to face with the reality that Barnabas might not be welcome in her circles. His sun-toughened coloring and thick black hair would draw some stares. His precise use of English, though fluent, would seem artificial. Becca might be comfortable at home in her own culture, but Barnabas would not be.

Though they had spoken on the radio and exchanged several letters, Becca and Barnabas had not seen each other since her impulsive jaunt to the capital. Eight weeks had passed and Barnabas simply could not get away. Between the language tutoring and his cassette work, he was busy every minute of the day. But Becca had managed to arrange a long weekend and had waited patiently for a seat on the plane, twice yielding it to someone with more urgent circumstances. This time she was determined to get on the plane. In a few hours, she would be sitting and talking with him again.

Becca sat at the desk in her classroom double-checking her lesson plans for her return. Her small bag was already packed, and she was idling right then, checking her watch every few minutes and waiting for a reasonable time to start the hike for the airstrip.

She closed her black lesson plan book and tucked it in her desk drawer just as the screen door squeaked open. Jill came in.

"Hi!" Becca greeted her.

"Hi." Jill gave Becca a half-smile, the most she ever gave. "Mom said you're going to Katmandu to see Barnabas."

"That's right."

"I think it's cool that you guys are getting married."

"Thanks, Jill."

"Is Barnabas going to take the pilot training?"

"We hope so. I have to get a job first, so we can save some money for the tuition."

"His family won't help?"

"Nope. We're on our own."

"Oh."

"We'll be fine, Jill. Don't worry about us."

"Are you really coming back here?"

"That's the plan. Barnabas has always planned to come back. That's the whole reason for the pilot training.

Jill was quiet. "Things sure have changed since you first came."

Becca chuckled. "They sure have."

"I was so jealous of you then, because you could leave if you wanted to. At the most, you had to be here only a year."

"I remember."

"Now you're going to come back and live here. That's really wild." They laughed together.

"Do you still want to go to the States?" Becca probed.

Jill quickly shook her head. "Not until I'm ready for college. Until then, I have things I want to do here."

Becca smiled. "I was hoping you would say that."

On her way down the mountain to the airstrip, Becca chuckled again at the change she had undergone in the last ten months. Jill was not the only one who had found purpose in making risky choices.

❧

When Becca stepped out of the little airplane in Katmandu and unfolded herself to her full height, Barnabas was there. He leaned against his motorcycle, holding two helmets and grinning. "I have a gift for you," he said, holding out a shiny white helmet.

"How romantic." Becca took the helmet and inspected it. "But Barnabas, I have never ridden on a motorcycle before."

"If you are going to live in this country, you must learn to ride a motorcycle."

"Will it matter if I say my father would not approve?"

He shook his head. "He does not yet understand our ways." He took the helmet from her hands and set it on her head. "Make sure the strap is snug."

Becca remembered how hesitant she was to get into a rundown taxi when she first arrived. Riding a motorcycle was a further extreme. But she surrendered her small bag to be strapped onto the back of the bike and then she climbed on behind Barnabas. Unabashedly, she wrapped her arms around his waist and settled her head on one shoulder. The engine roared and he pulled into traffic. At first Becca kept her eyes closed, fearful of seeing cows and pedestrians and gasping buses from a distance of only two inches. Gradually, she opened her eyes to watch Barnabas maneuver past obstacles and make steady progress across town. She relaxed, realizing that she had never felt safer than in his care.

Twenty minutes later, they pulled up in front of the mission guest house, where Becca had reserved a room for the next four nights. Harriett Metcalf greeted them at the door.

"Why, Rebecca Masterson, never in my wildest imagination would I have thought you would ride a motorcycle."

Becca laughed. "I'll stay at the passenger phase for a while, I'm sure."

"I used to have one, you know."

"You? A motorcycle?"

"For years. It's actually much more convenient than a car." Harriett opened the door. "Come on in, and I'll fix you some tea."

They followed her to one of the round, dining room tables. "I must say, the news of your engagement took us by surprise, but we are quite delighted for you."

"Thank you," Barnabas said. "We have some details to work out, but we are at peace about our decision." He looked toward Becca for confirmation and she nodded.

Harriett poured the tea, thick with milk and sugar in the Nepali style. "I don't know very much about your plans. When is the wedding?"

"Becca wants to get married in the U.S.," Barnabas said, "a few weeks after we arrive."

"I've already written to my mother to begin the arrangements," Becca explained. "I don't want a big fancy wedding, but I would like my family to be there. It might help them. . ."

"To accept your decision?" Harriett speculated.

Becca nodded.

"When will you begin your training, Barnabas?"

He and Becca glanced at each other. "We are uncertain about that."

"I thought you had already been accepted."

"I have. . .but the fees."

"Oh, I see."

Becca jumped in. "I'm going to get a teaching job, but it's hard to do that in a new state from this faraway. So he may not be able to start right away."

"And if I don't begin in September," Barnabas added, "I'll have to reapply and hope I get in next year."

Becca turned to him, startled. "I didn't know that!"

"I received a letter last week. They have had many applications and they say they cannot keep my spot open indefinitely. I must tell them soon of my intentions."

Becca tried not to let her shoulders sag. "Tell them you're coming. I'll just work harder at getting a job. It doesn't have to be teaching. I worked in an office during college."

Harriett set her teacup down. "So these are some of the details you still have to work out?"

They sat somberly over their tea. Harriett offered a plate of cookies. When the phone rang, Harriett reached behind her and answered it. She spoke briefly in Nepali and turned back to her guests.

"Barnabas, that was your literature office. They said your uncle is there."

"My uncle? Krishna?" His back stiffened.

"What is it, Barnabas?"

"I have not heard from anyone in my family for two months. They were very angry with me. If my uncle is looking for me, he must have bad news."

"You can't be sure of that," Becca said.

"I can think of no other reason. I must go."

"I'll go with you."

❧

Without flinching, Becca strapped on her helmet and straddled the bike like she had been doing it for years. They zipped across town. Hanging on to his waist, Becca could feel the tension in Barnabas's body.

Krishna stood outside the small, ground-floor apartment that served as the office for Barnabas's work. Barnabas hardly took time to park the bike.

"Uncle! What is it?"

"Nephew, why are you alarmed?" Krishna's voice was calm.

"Why are you here?" Barnabas's alarm was not eased.

"To see you, of course."

"I'm sorry, Uncle, but I did not expect—"

"Do you think the whole family has thrown you out for good?"

"My father told me not to come home again."

Krishna nodded. "If I were you, I would not go home just yet." He glanced at Becca, who was standing behind Barnabas and had not spoken.

Barnabas scrambled for his manners and reached for her hand. "I'm sorry, Uncle. Do you remember meeting Rebecca?"

Becca stepped forward. "It's nice to see you again."

"I am delighted at this opportnity. It is an unexpected but pleasurable surprise." He bowed his head slightly toward her.

"So my parents are well?" Barnabas jumped back in and got back to the point. "And my sisters?"

"Everyone is in good health, I can assure you. Your mother, of course, is behaving in a dramatic way about your decision to marry an American."

"Dramatic?"

Krishna waved his hand. "Your mother loves you, Nephew. She is my sister and I know her well. She cannot turn her back on you for long."

"But my father—"

"He said what he said to please your mother at the moment."

"I don't know, Uncle Krishna. They were very angry. It is a disgrace to them that I have become a Christian, and now, to marry outside the village. . ."

"These are serious subjects," Krishna acknowledged. "We have all had difficulty understanding your choices. But I am here to say that I believe our family is stronger than these traditions. I will be a bridge between you and your family."

Becca held her breath and kept listening.

"A bridge?" Barnabas echoed.

"You have chosen your path out of a greater love. This is an admirable thing. Your mother has not yet realized that she raised her son to be a man of character. But I see it very clearly."

"Thank you, Uncle. I'm not sure what to say."

"Your reasons for being a pilot are a mystery to me, yet I admire your determination. You will be a fine pilot."

Becca squeezed Barnabas's hand.

"My business has been going very well," Krishna continued. "Your tuition is quite high by the standards of our country, but as long as business keeps up, I should be able to afford it."

"Uncle! What are you saying?"

Becca gasped.

Krishna laughed. "What do you think I am saying? I will pay your school fees."

"Thank the Lord!" Becca murmured.

"But, Uncle, why? Why would you pay for my training so that I can do something you do not believe in?"

"Because I believe in my nephew. You should be rewarded, not punished, for acting on conviction."

"How can I ever show my gratitude?"

"Be a great pilot. I must go now. I have a dinner engagement. Send me the papers from your school and I will make the arrangements."

Krishna's next motion was to hail a taxi. Becca and Barnabas were left, standing and staring at each other.

"Did that really happen?" Becca asked, hardly able to speak. "Was he really here?"

"He was here and quickly gone. That is the way of my uncle."

"The Lord blesses in unusual ways," Becca said, regaining her composure.

"Yes," Barnabas agreed. "This truly is God's blessing. For if we can reach my uncle, we can reach my family. Our God is a God of hope."

Becca looked around her. She stood in front of a small,

delapidated brick building on a narrow, unpaved street. She had been riding on a second-hand motorcycle around one of the dirtiest cities in the world. But somewhere beyond the pollution that thickened the air were the Himalaya Mountains with their glistening peaks. This is where she would spend her life. And, yes, her heart was full of hope for what the future would bring.

A Letter To Our Readers

Dear Reader:

In order that we might better contribute to your reading enjoyment, we would appreciate your taking a few minutes to respond to the following questions. When completed, please return to the following:

Rebecca Germany, Managing Editor
Heartsong Presents
P.O. Box 719
Uhrichsville, Ohio 44683

1. Did you enjoy reading *Nepali Noon*?
   - ❑ Very much. I would like to see more books by this author!
   - ❑ Moderately
     I would have enjoyed it more if ______________

     ____

2. Are you a member of **Heartsong Presents**? ❑Yes ❑No
   If no, where did you purchase this book? ______________

   ____

3. What influenced your decision to purchase this book? (Check those that apply.)

❑ Cover	❑ Back cover copy
❑ Title	❑ Friends
❑ Publicity	❑ Other______________

4. How would you rate, on a scale from 1 (poor) to 5 (superior), the cover design? ______________

5. On a scale from 1 (poor) to 10 (superior), please rate the following elements.

___Heroine ___Plot

___Hero ___Inspirational theme

___Setting ___Secondary characters

6. What settings would you like to see covered in **Heartsong Presents** books?___________________

____

____

7. What are some inspirational themes you would like to see treated in future books?_______________

____

____

8. Would you be interested in reading other **Heartsong Presents** titles? ❑ Yes ❑ No

9. Please check your age range:

❑ Under 18 ❑ 18-24 ❑ 25-34

❑ 35-45 ❑ 46-55 ❑ Over 55

10. How many hours per week do you read? __________

Name ___________________________________

Occupation ______________________________

Address ___________________________________

City_______________State__________Zip__________

Susannah Hayden

✿❀✿❀✿❀✿❀✿❀✿❀✿❀✿❀✿❀✿❀✿❀✿❀✿❀✿❀✿❀✿❀✿

__*A Matter of Choice*—Stacie's new job promotion could mean the end of her future with Brad. . .or the start of a new and perhaps better life with Dillon. What life is Stacie to have? HP14

__*Between Love and Loyalty*—Megan Browning and her friends are working frantically to keep the old Homestead Youth Camp running. Then Megan discovers that the young architect who has captured her heart is planning on developing Homestead into condominiums. HP69

__*The Road Before Me*—Overwhelmed by self-doubt, Julie Covington searches for an answer. At her grandmother's childhood home in Maine she finds comfort and solace in the writings of a young girl, a girl who walked the same road as the one before Julie. HP77

__*Between the Memory and the Moment*—Jenna seems happy living and working at the camp owned by Dillon Graves. After all, she's hopelessly in love with the much-older Dillon, and he genuinely appreciates her work. Still, Jenna feels compelled to move on. But to what? HP113

__*Farther Along the Road*—Julie Covington wants to be accepted as a serious artist, and she wants to possess a love as vital as the one her grandmother had for her first love. When Larry Paxton displays interest in her paintings, Julie begins to feel hopeful that both needs can be fulfilled. HP117

Send to: Heartsong Presents Reader's Service
P.O. Box 719
Uhrichsville, Ohio 44683

Please send me the items checked above. I am enclosing **$2.95** for *each* title, totaling $________(please add $1.00 to cover postage and handling per order. OH add 6.25% tax. NJ add 6% tax.).
Send check or money order, no cash or C.O.D.s, please.
To place a credit card order, call 1-800-847-8270.

NAME ____

ADDRESS ____

CITY/STATE ______________________________ ZIP ____________

HAYDEN